Palgrave Studies in Institutions, Economics and Law

Law and Economics is an interdisciplinary field of research that has emerged in recent decades, with research output increasing dramatically and academic programmes in law and economics multiplying. Increasingly, legal cases have an economic dimension and economic matters depend on rules and regulations. Increasingly, economists have realized that "institutions matter" because they influence economic activities. Increasingly, too, economics is used to improve our understanding of how institutions and how legal systems work. This new Palgrave Pivot series studies the intersection between law and economics, and addresses the need for greater interaction between the two disciplines.

More information about this series at
http://www.palgrave.com/gp/series/15241

Bora Altay · Fuat Oğuz

# Rules, Contracts and Law Enforcement in the Ottoman Empire

## The Case of Tax-Farming Contracts

palgrave macmillan

Bora Altay
Department of Economics
Ankara Yıldırım Beyazıt University
Ankara, Turkey

Fuat Oğuz
Department of Economics
Ankara Yıldırım Beyazıt University
Ankara, Turkey

ISSN 2662-6535 ISSN 2662-6543 (electronic)
Palgrave Studies in Institutions, Economics and Law
ISBN 978-3-030-79576-4 ISBN 978-3-030-79577-1 (eBook)
https://doi.org/10.1007/978-3-030-79577-1



This Palgrave Macmillan imprint is published by the registered company Springer Nature Switzerland AG
The registered company address is: Gewerbestrasse 11, 6330 Cham, Switzerland

# Contents

# List of Figures

# List of Tables

CHAPTER 1

# Introduction

**Abstract** This chapter presents the main purpose of the study that focuses on the role of institutions and law over the economic performance of the Ottoman Empire during the early modern period. In this sense, tax-farming institutions and the legal structure of the Ottoman Empire are at the center of this study. A long-standing assumption of the recent literature is that efficient institutions in establishing cooperation are achieved to direct financial resources toward productive activities. The economic growth and divergence follow the evolution of institutions. On the other hand, our results show that the Ottoman rulers lost their absolute power during the evolution of tax-farming institutions. The long-standing presumptions argue that the Ottoman sultans as other Muslim rulers had absolute power for several reasons, the game-theoretical perspective shows that contractual relations could not satisfy neither Pareto efficiency nor Pareto inefficient equilibrium(s) or outcome(s). Instead, the Ottoman Empire is between these two equilibria due to the lack of absolute power of the state. It is shown that the powerful groups achieved to limit the power of the state, or the institutional structure promoted partial rule of law in the Ottoman Empire. The partial rule of law, however, entails limited economic growth according to competing European societies.



B. Altay and F. Oğuz, *Rules, Contracts and Law Enforcement in the Ottoman Empire*, Palgrave Studies in Institutions, Economics and Law, https://doi.org/10.1007/978-3-030-79577-1_1

**Keywords** Institutions · Institutional change · The rule of law · Contracts · Law enforcement

Economic analysis of law has become a major tool to understand and analyze economic history since the 1990s. The methodological advances of game theory and its applications to historical contexts provide more insights into economic rationale in pre-modern societies. The perspective of the economic analysis of law is enriched by the concepts of the new institutional economics such as transaction costs and credible commitments. Individuals in history are not different from moderns in terms of their self-interested behaviors. While institutional constraints differ across societies, the basic motive of human beings remains the same. This work looks into Ottoman society to understand the motives and institutional environment of tax-farming contracts.

The beginning of the first industrial revolution changed societies and disrupted the traditional economic activities around the world beginning with Europe. The pre-modern world of transition created a new economic system around the world. In line with the transformation of other societies, the Ottoman Empire experienced a series of exogenous shocks, endogenous problems, institutional changes, and political crises before the nineteenth century. The collapse of the traditional order created openings for new institutions, as economic actors searched for less-costly alternatives to old institutions. New institutions were tested within its large territories as military, political, and economic actors struggled over conflicting interests. These institutional changes and their effects on the Ottoman economic performance are the subjects of this book.

This period is known as the beginning of economic stagnation and decline in Ottoman society. There is now a substantial literature on the Ottoman economy and institutions. While most research focuses on the effects of exogenous factors beyond the control of economic actors, a few others draw attention to the role of endogenous changes, including non-economic institutions as the structure of agents and the law. Some historians refer to diverse inferences on the institutional change and its effects on the political and economic order in the Ottoman society. However, there are not many in-depth studies in this area.

Failure of the fiscal system has long been argued as the main reason for the change in Ottoman economic history. The history of the Ottoman

Empire from the sixteenth and to the nineteenth century is more complex than a simple failure in fiscal institutions. This period includes institutional changes in fiscal institutions as well as shifting coalitions and changing the balance of power among elites. While both Western European societies and the Ottoman Empire developed similar institutional mechanisms, their institutional differences caused economic divergence during the pre-industrial era. We study non-economic institutions along with economic ones to understand the divergence between the West and the Ottomans.

Fiscal institutions are at the core of Ottoman economic activity. The finance of state activities and wars was always a priority. Decentralized economic activities in distant regions were seen as part of the model that supported the central government. Maximizing state revenues was the main purpose to finance increasing costs of changing economic and political environments. During the early modern period, financing costs depended on how effective the decentralized mechanisms were. The effectiveness of revenue extracting was the outcome of small institutional differences. From the beginning of the sixteenth century, the divergence emerged in state revenues and per capita tax income among European societies and the Ottoman Empire.

This book focuses on fiscal institutions (the tax-farming institutions), the structure of agents, and the structure of law during the pre-industrial period to study the complex nature of institutional change and economic performances. This era shows that the Ottoman Empire and its administrative structure changed toward a more decentralized structure. In turn, judicial/religious-based agents (state agents) and powerful provincial notables (non-state agents) increased their power through tax-farming contracts and state offices of law enforcement. Both of these groups developed new mechanisms to become active participants in governance. They trumped the dominance of the privileged military/administrative-based agents.

The traditional *timar* institution surrounded the political and economic structures of the Ottoman Empire. The institution of timar became a highly centralized structure and was used extensively by the state. It was based on contractual relations between the central authority and its military/administrative-based agents. Timar contracts were also based on mutual trust among contracting parties. They allowed military/administrative-based agents to influence the political opinions of the central authority (sultans). In turn, shifting coalitions and changing alliances started to emerge through tax-farming contracts. The newly created alliances and coalitions resisted innovations that would crop their shares from tax revenues. During the pre-industrial period, coalitions, and alliances of judicial/religious-based agents and provincial notables dominated the tax-farming contract market and state offices.

During the pre-industrial period, Western European societies faced similar crises. However, institutional differences between the European societies and the Ottoman society gave way to diverging solutions. One of the most explicit responses of the central authority was to establish coalitions and alliances through tax-farming contracts. Tax-farming institutions and their mechanisms were tested during the last two centuries before the nineteenth century. The role of judicial/religious-based agents and provincial notables, however, continued to increase their power over the tax-farming contract market and the law. Western European rulers, on the other side, established coalitions and partnerships with the agents from economically powerful groups such as merchants. In this sense, the Ottoman Empire experienced different versions of contractual relations, law enforcement, and top-down mechanisms during the pre-industrial period.

Why did some societies become richer, and others remained backward even before industrialization? This question remains the primary subject matter of the literature. Institutions were instrumental in allocating financial resources toward productive, unproductive, and destructive areas throughout history. More importantly, institutional structures included not only economic mechanisms but also non-economic ones. Institutions consisted of formal and informal rules that created incentive mechanisms of decision-makers within economic and political environments. Formal rules comprised constitutions, laws, codes, and other written rules while informal rules consisted of cultural beliefs, traditions, norms, and other kinds of unwritten rules. The main purposes of institutions were to sustain order and reduce uncertainty as well as reducing transaction costs.

The structure of the law was one of the most important critical junctures over the economic divergence during the pre-industrial period. Even if the societies imposed written rules and courts as the main organizations, small institutional differences entailed diverse enforcement mechanisms that determine why some societies established welfare-enhancing institutions and others did not during the pre-industrial period.

The institutional change and shifting coalitions were crucial to understanding the economic performances. They were also the reasons behind the relative backwardness, including the structure of law and the rule of law contexts. The rule of law, in a historical context, was a process, in which all societies had to satisfy certain conditions and experience unsuccessful contractual relations on the way of establishing efficient legal structures that promoted welfare-enhancing economic structures. The recent literature on the rule of law argued that the legal structure and its mechanisms are given and exogenous factors within the economic structures. A few of those emphasized that the rule of law was an endogenous dynamic and changed over time regarding changing circumstances within the economic and political structures.

The concept of the rule of law is related to the relationship between the "state" and society in the historical context. The "state" means the rulers, kings, or sultans, who had absolute power over the violence during the pre-industrial period. It is commonly known that the state had absolute power over decision-making in economic and political life in the Ottoman Empire. The Ottoman rulers imposed not only the Sharia Law but also *Urfi* Law (Sultanic Law) to sustain the orders in the empire. The *Urfi* Law is based on traditions and norms, in which the rulers could bend the Sharia law. Since the principles of the Sharia Law needed to be interpreted, local conditions played a major role in the implementation of tax-farming contracts and adjudication of conflicts.

This study has focused on the role of *Urfi* Law on the economic performance of the Ottoman Empire. The Sharia Law is related to the rule of law in which the law enforcement was efficient in imposing the rules to each party, including the sultan or the central authority. The historical evidence has indicated that it was difficult to establish the rule of law due to the monopoly power of the central authority in creating violence. The primary obstacle in front of this is the *Urfi Law* that the central authority applies by using its power. Through tax-farming contracts, this study has revealed a systematic and theoretical analysis to test effects of *rule by law* in answering the proposed questions above.

The term of institution represents the rules of the game from this point. These include not only formal rules but also informal rules within the economic structure. The term of rules, however, shows the written conditions in tax farming contracts that show how the game should be played. Finally, the concept of law refers to the sum of the rules created depending on the traditions in the Ottoman Empire. The main issue in these concepts is the rules of the game, which are changed by the central authority according to the exogenous shocks and endogenous dynamics. In other words, this study presumes that the Sharia Law (the rule of law) and rules are difficult to apply and that only the rules of the game change according to the circumstances.

The tax-farming institutions and their mechanisms can be used to study the changing balance of power between the state and its agents. Tax-farming institutions as a nexus of contracts provide tools for analyzing why the Ottoman Empire failed to establish the rule of law. Furthermore, the question of why the Ottoman Empire failed, even though it came close to establishing the rule of law is one of the most important deficiencies of the current literature. Although the recent literature argues that the partial rule of law exists within the institutional environment, the analysis focuses on law enforcement over individuals instead of the direct involvement of the state.

We analyze economic performance and the structure of law in the Ottoman Empire through the concept of the rule of law. The concept of the rule of law, however, has contained complex and broad meanings. One of the recent researches has defined the rule of law as it entails government accountability, open access to the legal and political process, unbiased and efficient judicial decisions, well-defined laws and rules as well as stable laws, and the protection of human rights (Kuran, 2010, p. 71). This study has used the concept of the rule of law in a more limited scope. The historical perspective focused on the rule of law has argued that the rule of law was crucial to limit the coercive power of rulers and forced decision-makers to honor their commitments within economic exchanges (North & Weingast, 1989; Root, 1989). This study, in this sense, has considered the rule of law as limiting the coercive power of the Ottoman central authority within contractual relations. As it is mentioned above, the *Urfi Law* was the main obstacle on the emergence of the rule of law.

Tax-farming contracts allow the establishment of the path of strategies and choices of the state during the pre-industrial period. These contracts were used to extract revenue and to share political power. In these contracts, the state could choose to delegate representative agents for limited periods. Law enforcement became a crucial determinant in establishing the rule of law over defecting contracts. Although absolute power of the state existed in contractual relations, the historical data shows that the state exercised its power selectively for certain tax-farming contracts. The state resorted to its absolute power in about half of the existing contracts.

In addition to contract durations, changing prices over tax-farming contracts provide another tool for analyzing the rule of law in the Ottoman Empire. The allocation of tax-farming contracts was based on an auction mechanism, in which the agents who were offered the highest price can obtain state offices. Although the state had an incentive to transfer contracts when received a higher price offer, our analysis of these contracts shows the state chose to transfer the contract before the intended duration with the same or lower prices to a new agent. These types of transactions can be observed in approximately half of the contracts. Thus, the contract durations and prices provide explicit data for quantitative analysis on the rule of law in the Ottoman Empire.

This book is organized around two main objectives. The first is to determine why the Ottoman Empire failed to establish the rule of law in an institutional context. Our primary sources of data are tax-farming contracts from different regions of the Ottoman Empire from the beginning of the sixteenth century to the nineteenth century. We extract intended durations, actual durations, and prices of contracts. Each tax-farming contract we employ includes complete information to identify simple patterns over changing strategies and perceptions of contracting parties. In other words, these contracts are sufficient to follow the evolutionary process of contracts as well as law enforcement.

The second objective is to show the level of rule of law and equilibrium(s) that emerged within the contractual relations through the structure of law. We employ game-theoretical models to estimate the trend of the rule of law in the Ottoman Empire. This path will show at what point the Ottoman Empire failed to establish the rule of law. In analyzing the rule of law, we also employ specific conditions that are compatible with historical context among many perspectives, following the work by Douglass North, John Wallis, and Barry R. Weingast (2009).[1]

To achieve these two objectives, this book includes the following chapters. Chapter 2 discusses the role of institutions and the rule of law in a historical context. The recent literature on the role of institutions shows that better economic performances were the outcome of welfare-enhancing institutions and efficient mechanisms during the pre-industrial period. This period is characterized by the domination of decentralized

[1] From this point, NWW approach.

institutions in the economic structure of both Western European societies and the Ottoman Empire.

The literature shows that the influence of non-economic institutions started to increase while the decentralized institutions were dominating the economic structures. In this sense, contracting parties shared not only economic privileges but also political powers through contracts. As long as the states are permanent parties of these contracts, the rule of law has its importance in economic performances. In this sense, the second chapter continues with the historical background of how the rule of law emerged in the first place. The historical examples show that the structure of law should be accepted as endogenous. In other words, the structure of law and its enforcement mechanisms determine the path of judicial decisions and their evolution over time. As the structure of the law changes, economic and political decisions adapt to the new legal environment. Finally, this chapter integrates the theoretical and historical background of the institutions and the rule of law into the Ottoman Empire through the historical background of the tax-farming institutions.

Chapter 3 studies the historical background of the structure of law in the Ottoman Empire. Although the recent literature examines the relationship between the rule of law and the power of Muslim rulers in Islamic societies, the Ottoman Empire had a different and complex legal structure during the pre-industrial period. We show that the rules were enforced under two different laws: Sharia Law (Religious Law) and *Urfi* Law (Sultanic Law).

The rules in Sharia Law are fixed and difficult to change. The *Urfi* Law, however, consists of rules that can be changed by the willingness of the sultans. As it is given below, the Ottoman sultans only could change the rules of law within traditions. Limited ability to change the rules allows decisions to evolve. Thus, the third chapter focuses on the evolutionary process in judicial decisions and changing rules regarding the *Urfi* Law, surrounding contractual relations within the tax-farming institutions.

Chapter 4 focuses on economic indicators to examine the economic performance of the Ottoman Empire during the pre-industrial period. Despite the lack of data for developing economies before industrialization, tax revenues provide sufficient information to understand long-term economic performances. As it is given below, the tax-farming institutions surrounded a substantial part of tax revenues in the Ottoman Empire. The efficiency of these institutions determines the level of tax revenues. Their effectiveness allows a comparative analysis of the institutions of societies through per capita tax revenues. We use per capita GDP levels to offer a comparative perspective on the institutional structures and economic performances of the Ottoman Empire.

Chapter 5 gives the legal structure of tax-farming contracts, including prices, contract durations, conditions, and liabilities of contracting parties. Furthermore, Chapter 5 presents the structure of agents and their changes from the beginning of the sixteenth century to the nineteenth century. The changing structure of agents is a reflection of changing institutional structures and the level of the rule of law. In short, this chapter gives the rules of the game that determine the basis of quantitative and theoretical perspectives in the following chapters.

Chapter 6 presents a descriptive analysis of the tax-farming institutions, including prices, annual payments, regions, and other economic variables in contracts. The prices and annual payments given in contracts are in Ottoman currencies. The raw data reflects nominal values. To obtain more accurate data, each variable will be converted into real values in terms of silver with the prices of 1913. Following the descriptive analysis, Chapter 7 gives game-theoretical models of tax-farming contracts to examine the level of the rule of law in the Ottoman Empire. We employ tools from Prisoner's Dilemma (PD) game for two reasons. First, the PD game is a simple embodiment of establishing cooperation in contractual relations. In this sense, the PD game generates the basis of our theoretical perspective to analyze equilibrium(s) and outcome(s) as well as the rule of law.

Our results are related to the literature on the role of institutions and their effects on the relative backwardness of developing societies. A long-standing assumption of the recent literature is that efficient institutions in establishing cooperation are achieved to direct financial resources toward productive activities. The economic growth and divergence follow the evolution of institutions. On the other hand, our results show that the Ottoman rulers lost their absolute power during the evolution of tax-farming institutions. The long-standing presumptions argue that the Ottoman sultans as other Muslim rulers had absolute power for several reasons. As it is given below, the game-theoretical perspective shows that contractual relations could satisfy neither Pareto efficiency nor Pareto inferior equilibrium(s) or outcome(s). Instead, the Ottoman Empire is between these two equilibria due to the lack of absolute power of the state. It is shown that the powerful groups achieved to limit the power of the state, or the institutional structure promoted partial rule of law in the Ottoman Empire.

## References

Kuran, T. (2010). The rule of law in Islamic thought and practice: A historical perspective. In J. J. Heckman, R. L. Nelson, & L. Cabatingan (Eds.), *Global perspectives on the rule of law* (pp. 71–89). Routledge.

North, D. C., Wallis, J. J., & Weingast, B. R. (2009). *Violence and social orders: A conceptual framework for interpreting recorded human history*. Cambridge University Press.

North, D. C., & Weingast, B. (1989). Constitutions and commitment: The evolution of institutions governing public choice in seventeenth-century England. *Journal of Economic History, 49*(4), 803–832.

Root, H. L. (1989). Tying the King's hands: Credible commitment and royal fiscal policy during the old regime. *Rationality and Society, 1*(2), 240–258.

CHAPTER 2

# The Rule of Law and Role of Institutions in the Historical Context

**Abstract** This chapter discusses the role of institutions and the rule of law in a historical context. The recent literature on the role of institutions argues that better economic performances emerged from welfare-enhancing institutions and efficient mechanisms during the pre-industrial period. This period is characterized by the domination of decentralized institutions in the economic structure of both Western European societies and the Ottoman Empire. The early modern period has also been characterized by contractual relations between the rulers (kings, lords, princes, sultans, etc.) and powerful groups. The cooperation among contracting parties has been a major driving force of economic progress. The theoretical background based on the rule of law context has included historical and institutional literature. This literature has been crucial to understanding how some societies solved credible commitment and the law enforcement problems and how others failed over time. Furthermore, the literature has presented how institutions did change over time. The theoretical background has shown that the Ottoman Empire developed institutions, and these institutions emerged for the same purpose under the rules of the game. We have shown that the institutional change that emerged in the Ottoman Empire is compatible with collective action theories.



B. Altay and F. Oğuz, *Rules, Contracts and Law Enforcement in the Ottoman Empire*, Palgrave Studies in Institutions, Economics and Law, https://doi.org/10.1007/978-3-030-79577-1_2

**Keywords** Institutions · Game-theoretical perspectives · Institutional change · Pre-industrial period · Collective action theory

The growing literature over the role of institutions includes a significant number of definitions. Societies have different technological and non-technological features. It is common to refer to the latter as institutions (Greif, 2006, p. 5). The technological features emerge from different geographical locations, organizations on capital accumulation, and knowledge that is based on diverse mental models of individuals. Non-technological features include cultural beliefs, traditions, norms, the structure of law, and law enforcement models. Institutional differences affect decisions on economic and political choices (Greif, 2006; North, 1990).

Examining the role of institutions over economic performances, three distinct views have dominated the recent literature: "institutions-as-rules", "institutions-as-equilibria" and "institutions-as-players" (Aoki, 2001, p. 5). In institutions-as-players view institutions as organizations or players of the game (Nelson, 1994, p. 57). The other two views, however, have a more complex understanding of the role of institutions. Douglass North (1990, pp. 3–4) defines institutions as humanly devised constraints that generate human interactions and determine incentive mechanisms. The devised constraints and incentives are based on formal and informal rules of the societies. In other words, written and unwritten rules form the rules of the game by which all players abide. Each society develops different institutions as economic, political, and religious, and each of them determines the "game" played between the state and their agents (Rubin, 2017, p. 12). The strategies and choices of players emerge from the rules of the game, and these are significant for building an institutional theory. The rules of the game determine the boundaries of players, and this is crucial to reduce uncertainty within the institutions-as-rules perspective (North, 1990, p. 6). Once a player faces too much uncertainty, this agent will either avoid transacting or will choose to be decisive to increase gains in the short run. As William H. Riker (1982, p. 4) indicates that institutions are rules about the behaviors of players and making decisions. The strategies that promote short-run gains reduce efficient economic choices and increase transaction costs. In this sense, the major role of institutions is to decrease transaction costs in an economy by determining the rules. As it is given in Ronald Coase's (1960) main argument, when transactions are costly, institutions matter. Oliver Williamson (1975) carries a step further transaction costs approach, including contracts and contracting parties into the institutional structure.

The institutions-as-rules perspective investigates the evolutionary and repeated games (Aoki, 2001; Bowles, 2009; Sugden, 1986). In most cases, traditional behaviors evolve without any third-party enforcement. When a tradition emerges, agents will change specific features due to evolutionary pressures. Thus, traditions and their associated characteristics evolve together. Traditions can be coded into the legal structure to prevent increasing costs from opportunistic behaviors of the players. Robert Sugden (1986, p. 5) points out that the law can be described as reflections of the codes of conduct that are imposed by humans on them. This version of the institutions-as-rules perspective suggests that there is no need for a third-party enforcer or governance structures to enforce rules. Instead, the rules of the game are predetermined by traditions, norms, beliefs, and codes of conduct, which prevent humans from moving toward unproductive behavior and strategies. In this sense, the rules of the game generate self-enforcing mechanisms within the institutional environment. As it is given below, the contracts and their enforcements were based on this specific perspective of institutions-as-rules under the traditional *timar* institution. The *Urfi* Law incorporates traditions into the legal structure to establish mutual trust with administrative/military-based agents. Traditions coded in the legal structure are basic conditions for the state to sustain its political power over its subjects in the Ottoman Empire (Weber, 1954). The traditions also promote self-enforcing mechanisms for cooperation within the contractual relations.

Leonid Hurwicz (1993, 1996) defines institutions as an enforcement mechanism within institutions-as-rules perspective. The rules of the game determine who plays the game, what actions can be followed by the players, and what outcomes can emerge from the choice sets of each player. The key element is that rules must be enforceable. As North (2003) argues that the degree of enforcement in a society is one of the key determinants of economic performances through time. Hurwicz (1996) states that if self-enforceability does not work, the market needs an enforcement mechanism. These enforcement mechanisms should have the ability to alter the rules to increase the costs of being deceptive and payoff functions of each player. Law enforcement through third-party governance surrounds the tax-farming institution of the Ottoman Empire. The deterioration of cooperation under self-enforcing mechanisms entails institutional change toward the tax-farming institutions. The several reasons came from exogenous shocks and endogenous dynamics entail increasing costs in the traditional *timar* institution. The solution is to establish third-party governance to reduce costs of uncertainty and enforcement. But the outcome is that the agents controlling third-party governance changed rules regarding their interests within the new institutional structure.

Hurwicz's institutions-as-rules perspective brings equilibrium views of institutions out. Andrew Schotter (1981, p. 155) argues that institutions are equilibrium(s) of behaviors and conventions. The main problem is what players do under the rules of the game instead of what the rules are. Masahiko Aoki (2001, p. 7) divides the institutions-as-equilibrium perspective into two different approaches: the evolutionary game approach and the repeated game approach. Under the evolutionary game approach, conventions are crucial, and they become dominant strategies without any third-party mechanism. When conventions evolve, each player develops choice sets to sustain gains from transactions (Aoki, 2001; Bowles, 2006; Sugden, 1986). The repeated game approach, on the other side, depended on the concepts of equilibrium(s) such as subgame perfect equilibrium. The critical issue is the role of expectations of players, or the beliefs shared by the players. While the subgame perfect equilibrium creates a self-enforcing mechanism to keep each player honest, the outcomes without credible enforcement mechanisms cause inefficient equilibrium(s). If players believe that the gains from defection are higher than being honest, they will choose to defect whatever the other players choose to play. Thus, defection becomes the dominant strategy, and the outcome will be the equilibrium.

A subgame perfect equilibrium describes a strategy that is established by the players comprehensively. In other words, this equilibrium is precautions for possible contingencies that emerged from the opposite party. The strategies or equilibrium(s) also may never be observed in a game during the play. The absolute power of sultans and their confiscatory behaviors can be considered as a subgame perfect equilibrium. If agents behave honestly in contractual relations, confiscation may never emerge as an equilibrium (institution). Yet, it is commonly known that the state used its coercive power in contractual relations and confiscation became an explicit strategy. The agents, however, develop diverse mechanisms to limit the coercive power of the state. This process brings out that the institutions and their changes in the Ottoman Empire are compatible with the institutions-as-rules perspective because of its dynamic nature during the pre-industrial period.

The pre-industrial period is characterized by the dominance of decentralized institutions within the institutional environment of societies. In the absence of centralized political and legal institutions, societies employed decentralized institutions to mitigate the costs of transactions (Rubin, 2017, p. 16). Although the Ottoman Empire is considered a bureaucratized and centralized empire during the classical age (1300–1600), rapid territorial expansion directs the state to establish decentralized institutions, establishing representative bodies (Inalcık, 2018, p. 134; Karaman, 2009).

The rule of law, in the historical context, emerges within the decentralized institutions, in which principal-agent relations dominate the institutional environment. Principals delegate authority to agents to perform certain services, and once an agent is employed, principals face controlling problems (Kiser, 1999). The agents, however, face another problem based on the political power of principles that entails increasing risks in contractual relations. The principals hold two kinds of power in their hands. The states as principals have absolute power over the contractual relations because of their monopoly power on violence. The other kinds of principals, merchants, or the feudal lords have both political and economic powers to impose over agents. In principle, there are two main problems in principal-agent relations, (1) players' interests often differ from others' interests, (2) both principals and agents have better information about their actions in contractual relations (Kiser, 1999, p. 146).

Under these problems, principals have better financial resources to mitigate the costs of controlling agents. These groups could direct their financial resources to establish efficient monitoring mechanisms for controlling the actions of agents. The principals also have a chance to choose their agents among many unemployed agents. More importantly, principals have adequate financial resources to capture gains from defection, spreading a bad reputation about employed agents within the contractual relations. The agents, on the other hand, have better information about their actions and past behaviors. Once there is a lack of enforcement mechanisms in the market, agents prefer opportunistic behaviors in contractual relations. The agents, in such an environment, have incentives to act opportunistically before principals did. Thus, mutual defection will be the equilibrium, in which Pareto inefficient outcomes emerge.

The emergence of the rule of law concept is essentially based on solving these problems. The increasing density of long-distance trade from the eleventh century directs merchants to employ agents in commercial activities. The information and uncertainty problems force societies to develop institutional mechanisms to capture gains from cooperation. Avner Greif (1989, 1993, 1994, 2006) compares institutional mechanisms of two different societies—Genoese and Maghrib—in solving coordination and commitment problems through law enforcement. Each society has a lack of centralized authority to develop third-party governance such as courts. Maghrib merchants develop institutional mechanisms regarding informal rules while Genoese merchants employ formal rules to mitigate increasing costs of long-distance trade. The former establishes "coalitions", in which Maghrib merchants could hire agents from the members of the coalition. The coalition mitigates the costs of information about past behaviors of the agents. Once a member of the coalition attempts to cheat, the other members have a chance to acquire this information at low costs. The coalition, in this sense, directs both principals and agents to behave honestly.

The latter develops private courts (the Law Merchant) to mitigate increasing costs of information and uncertainty within the long-distance trade. These private courts have no authority to enforce the law. But they have mechanisms in providing information about past behaviors of the agents (Milgrom et al., 1990). In other words, if a merchant needs to acquire information about the agent hired before, courts provide information in exchange for a certain amount of fee. Once an opportunistic behavior of an agent or a merchant is recorded in private courts, they face losing their future expected benefits in contractual relations. In the rule of law context, these earlier mechanisms are developed to limit the opportunistic behaviors of players. During the following centuries, the emergence of more centralized political and legal structures entails complex relations in commercial activities. Instead of trading in different markets, merchants are obliged to trade in the lands of rulers, who have monopoly power on violence and the law.

The commercial game between the state and merchants may end in different forms. The state can impose its absolute power to confiscate the goods of merchants to capture the highest gains for one time in the short run. Or the state may promote the property rights of the merchants and secure these rights through its military power. Merchants, on the other side, choose to be honest by paying a share from gains as a tax or choose to renege on contracts by leaving territories of the state without paying any fee. Thus, merchants choose to establish "merchant guilds" and "boycott mechanisms" to limit the power of the state (Greif et al., 1994; Milgrom et al., 1990). These guilds can impose a boycott against the states with coercive power, and the boycott entails losses in gains from trade for the states. In sum, boycott mechanisms of guilds and coercive power of the state force contracting parties to behave honestly and promote cooperation that provides the highest gains from trade for both players. The rule of law directs each contracting party to behave honestly even if there is no third-party governance within the institutional environment. The private courts have no authority to enforce the law, but they direct players for cooperation by providing information about past behaviors at low costs. In other words, the rule of law as self-enforcing mechanisms achieve to limit opportunistic behavior of contracting parties by reducing uncertainty and costs of transactions.

The emergence of the rule of law, however, is an outcome of the institutional change process over time. Institutions do change. As it is existing for institutional structures, institutional change also has a different path for each society. According to North (1989, 1994), institutional change has three main sources: changes in relative prices, changes in perceptions of agents, and skills of the players. North (1989, p. 1325) adds that the role of changing military technology and efficient size of political structure induce fundamental changes in the economic structure. In this sense, the institutional change emerges endogenously or with third-party governance throughout history. Institutions are either designed in a coordinated manner by a coercive power or institutional change occurs spontaneously under uncoordinated choices. Therefore, institutions do change over time.

The recent literature argues the institutional change from different perspectives. The most common questions are which institutions do matter, and why and how do they change? Such theoretical questions are also related to changes in institutions of the Ottoman Empire during the early modern period. It is more common to examine institutional changes through exogenous shocks that consisted of the discovery of new trade routes, the flow of precious metals from the New World, and changing military technology. What the driving force of exogenous shocks is the changes in endogenous dynamics. As North (1990, p. 10) presents in *Institutions, Institutional Change and Economic Performance*, the perception of agents is the primary determinant of institutional change throughout history. Even before the exogenous shocks emerged during the early modern period, it is known that societies experienced a series of exogenous shocks. The adaptation of societies depends on the strategies the players produce against shocks. The perception of agents causes changes in *Rules*. The opportunity sets of decision-makers, however, determine the direction of changing rules. In this sense, it is comprehensible why some societies were more successful to adopt welfare-enhancing rules and others did not throughout history. The bounded rationality limits the choice sets of decision-makers in the process of changing the rules of the game. This study presents that the Ottoman Empire experienced a struggle between institutional change and bounded rationality during the early modern period (Chapter 4 and 5).

The institutional change in theoretical perspective mainly emerges in two different perspectives: *Collective Action Theories* and *Evolutionary Theories* (*Hayekian Perspectives*). Understanding these perspectives is crucial to understand how the rules changed in the Ottoman Empire, and why they caused the failure and economic divergence until the nineteenth century. These theories also allow us to examine changing rules incrementally. The structure of law, in this sense, is not taken as given. Instead, it is a part of the evolutionary process based on bargaining, negotiations, and choices of the players.

The tax-farming institution provides historical evidence to examine the role of changing rules over the economic performance of the Ottoman Empire. All interactions that emerged within the tax-farming institution are parts of the judicial process. The contractual relations are related not only to economic exchanges but also to judicial decisions. The legal structure determines the share of the central authority in financial resources. Even if the recent literature argues that the Ottoman rulers had absolute power over contractual relations, the legal structure and its evolutionary process of rules bring different stories out for the early modern period. Therefore, the structure of the law is the primary determinant of why the economic failures and divergence emerged in the Ottoman Empire.

Collective action theories have surrounded the literature on institutional change. The main driving forces are negotiations, bargaining, and political actions that alter the rules within the institutional environment. Gary Libecap (1989) argues that different property rights entail diverse outcome(s) and equilibrium(s) for societies. The decision-makers have determined the structure of property rights through their bargaining powers. Higher-level players have the power to change rules within the institutional environment. These groups can execute rule-changing activities. The contracting mechanisms emerge around the rules developed by groups who hold the power at one point. Libecap states that such contractual arrangements generate higher-level rules as well as the perception of agents. Thus, institutional change emerges from the process between rule-changing activities and the perception of agents. This kind of institutional change, however, emerges from exogenous shocks, and this process is path-dependent. Path dependency makes history matter.

Contrary to Libecap, Elinor Ostrom (2005) argues that institutional change emerges from both exogenous shocks and endogenous dynamics. The endogenous dynamics are crucial. The institutional environment includes some beneficiaries and losers from the change. In a historical context, beneficiaries hold off from compensating costs of losers. This is because beneficiaries consist of powerful groups in society. If beneficiaries can protect their interests, they prevent decision-makers from changing institutional structures toward efficient ones. Furthermore, beneficiaries force decision-makers to impose inefficient institutions which assures more gains for themselves.

The combination of beneficiaries and higher-level players (rules) are compatible with the structure of agents in the Ottoman Empire. As it is given below, the central authority established contractual relations with powerful groups, including military/administrative-based agents, judicial/religious-based agents, and provincial notables. The balance of power among these groups is flexible regarding changing economic and political environments. Under the collective action theories, these groups have the power to hinder welfare-enhancing changes and impose inefficient change through judicial decisions (Chapter 4 and 5). The institutional environment may not include an effective third-party governance mechanism to enforce "Coasian" bargaining that could clear the path.

Ostrom (2005) states that such institutional changes emerge from the bounded rationality of players that direct opportunistic behaviors within the contractual relations. Incorporating endogenous dynamics into the process of institutional change makes sense why some societies failed to change their institutions toward efficient ones. The problem is how powerful groups achieved to prevent mechanisms from changing toward new institutions for the efficient outcome(s) and equilibrium(s). The

State, political actors, judiciaries, and courts have a significant influence over institutional change when the "Coasian" bargaining is absent within the institutional environment. It can be argued that the Ottoman Empire had a lack of mechanisms for the "Coasian" bargaining. Thus, judicial decisions and courts should be incorporated into the analysis of economic performances through contractual relations.

Evolutionary theories include a different perspective rather than collective action theories (Kingston & Caballero, 2009). This perspective excludes central mechanisms (third-party governance) that determine the direction of institutional changes. The primary suggestion is that new rules of behavior extend efficient institutions while they entail the abandonment of inefficient ones (Alchian, 1950). The keys are uncoordinated actions and choices rather than a ruler's perceptions, collective choices, or political process. The competition is the driving force of institutional change. Williamson (2000) contributes to the role of transaction costs over institutional changes. Bounded rationality that promotes opportunistic behavior still exists within the evolutionary theories. It is, however, related to minimizing costs instead of preventing institutional change to maintain the interests of certain groups. In a world of positive transaction costs, the main purpose of players is to minimize costs within bounded rationality.

The transaction cost approach, however, includes deficiencies to explaining why some societies developed different rules for similar transactions, and why some societies failed to adopt more efficient institutions in the historical context. There is no explicit evidence on the costs of players within contractual relations in both France and the Ottoman Empire. Contrary to the market-oriented approaches of Alchian and Williamson, Friedrich A. Hayek (1973) argues that such questions could be solved by selection at the level of social groups. These groups practice and experience rules over time. This process allows them to displace inefficient institutions from the institutional environment under the process of selection mechanisms. Practices and experiences evolve through time. Hayek's "spontaneous order" indicates that rules evolve with the experiences of generations through time. These experiences create equilibrium strategies that are institutions. Societies, however, face coordination problems (Knight, 1995). One can suggest that even if societies could achieve established coordination among players, this was a historical accident (Young, 1996). Furthermore, Robert Sugden (1989) suggests that players generate mechanisms to coordinate strategies, but these can fail to establish efficient outcome(s) and equilibrium(s) for societies.

Institutional change begins with the perception of certain groups regarding both perspectives. Collective action theories put higher-level players at the center while evolutionary theories give importance to social groups. The primary difference is the role of the groups. The former has the power to determine the direction of institutional change and the latter does not. In either perspective, the emergence of efficient institutions depends on the coordinated strategies of players. The failure of coordination generates one of the problems of this study. We focus on higher-level players as certain social groups that surrounded the institutional environment of the Ottoman Empire. Their choices determine the direction of institutional change as well as economic growth during the early modern period.

## References


Alchian, A. (1950). Uncertainty, evolution and economic theory. *Journal of Political Economy, 58*(3), 211–221.

Aoki, M. (2001). *Toward a comparative institutional analysis*. The MIT Press.

Bowles, S. (2006). *Microeconomics: Behavior, institutions, and evolution*. Princeton: Princeton University Press.

Bowles, S. (2009). Did warfare among ancestral hunter-gatherers affect the evolution of human social behaviors? *Science, 324*, 1293–1298.

Coase, R. H. (1960). The problem of social cost. *Journal of Law and Economics, 3*, 1–44.

Greif, A. (1989). Reputation and coalition in medieval trade: Evidence on the Maghribi traders. *The Journal of Economic History, XLIX*(4), 857–882.

Greif, A. (1993). Contract enforceability and economic institutions in early trade: The Maghribi traders' coalition. *The American Economic Review, 83*(3), 525–548.

Greif, A. (1994). Cultural beliefs and the organization of society: A historical and theoretical reflection on collectivist and individualist societies. *The Journal of Political Economy, 102*(5), 912–950.

Greif, A. (2006). *Institutions and the path to the modern economy: Lessons from medieval trade*. Cambridge University Press.

Greif, A., Milgrom, P., & Weingast, B. R. (1994). Coordination, commitment and enforcement: The case of the merchant guild. *The Journal of Political Economy, 102*(4), 745–776.

Hayek, F. A. (1973). *Law, legislation and liberty, vol. 1: Rules and order*. University of Chicago Press.

Hurwicz, L. (1993). Toward a framework for analyzing institutions and institutional change. In S. Bowles, H. Gintis, & B. Gustafsson (Eds.), *Markets and democracy: Participation, accountability, and efficiency*. Cambridge University Press.

Hurwicz, L. (1996). Institutions as families of game forms. *Japanese Economic Review, 47*, 13–132.

Inalcık, H. (2018). *The Ottoman Empire: Sultan, society and economy*. Kronik.

Karaman, K. (2009). Decentralized coercion and self-restraint in provincial taxation: The Ottoman Empire, 15th–16th centuries. *Journal of Economic Behavior & Organization, 71*(3), 690–703.

Kingston, C., & Caballero, G. (2009). Comparing theories of institutional change. *The Journal of Institutional Economics, 5*(2), 151–180.

Kiser, E. (1999). Comparing varieties of agency theory in economics, political science, and sociology: An illustration from state policy implementation. *Sociological Theory, 17*(2), 146–170.

Knight, J. (1995). Models, interpretations and theories: Constructing explanations of institutional emergence and change. In J. Knight & I. Sened (Eds.), *Explaining social institutions*. University of Michigan Press.

Libecap, G. D. (1989). *Contracting for property rights*. Cambridge University Press.

Milgrom, P. R., North, D. C., & Weingast, B. (1990). The role of institutions the revival of trade: The medieval law merchant, private judges, and the champagne fairs. *Economics & Politics, 2*(1), 1–23.

Nelson, R. (1994). The co-evolution of technology, industrial structure, and supporting institutions. *Industrial and Corporate Change, 3*, 47–63.

North, D. C. (1989). Institutions and economic growth: An historical introduction. *World Development, 17*(9), 1319–1332.

North, D. C. (1990). *Institutions, institutional change and economic performance*. Cambridge University Press.

North, D. C. (1994). Economic performance through time. *The American Economic Review, 84*(3), 359–368.

North, D. C. (2003). The role of institutions in economic development. *United Nations Discussion Paper Series*, No. 2003.2, 1–10.

Ostrom, E. (2005). *Understanding institutional diversity*. Princeton University Press.

Riker, W. H. (1982). *Liberalism against populism: A confrontation between the theory of democracy and the theory of social choice*. W.H. Freeman.

Rubin, J. (2017). *Rulers, religion, and riches: Why the west got rich and the Middle East did not?* Cambridge University Press.

Schotter, A. (1981). *The economic theory of social institutions*. Cambridge University Press.

Sugden, R. (1986). New developments in the theory of choice under uncertainty. *Bulletin of Economic Research, 38*(1), 1–24.
Sugden, R. (1989). Spontaneous order. *The Journal of Economic Perspectives, 3*(4), 85–97.
Weber, M. (1954). *On law in economy and society* (E. Shils & M. Rheinstein, Trans.). Harvard University Press.
Williamson, O. E. (1975). *Markets and hierarchies: Analysis and antitrust implication*. The Free Press.
Williamson, O. E. (2000). The new institutional economics: Taking stock, looking ahead. *Journal of Economic Literature, 38*, 595–613.
Young, H. P. (1996). The economics of convention. *Journal of Economic Perspectives, 10*(2), 105–122.

CHAPTER 3

# The Relevance of the Rule of Law to the Ottoman Institutions: Historical Background

**Abstract** This chapter focuses on studies of the historical background of the structure of law in the Ottoman Empire. Although the recent literature examines the relationship between the rule of law and the power of Muslim rulers in Islamic societies, the Ottoman Empire had a different and complex legal structure during the pre-industrial period. We show that the rules were enforced under two different laws: Sharia Law (Religious Law) and *Urfi* Law (Sultanic Law). The rules in Sharia Law are fixed and difficult to change. The *Urfi* Law, however, consists of rules that can be changed by the willingness of the sultans. Ottoman sultans only could change the rules of law within traditions. Limited ability to change the rules allows decisions to evolve over time. Thus, the third chapter focuses on the evolutionary process in judicial decisions and changing rules regarding the *Urfi* Law, surrounding contractual relations within the tax-farming institutions.

**Keywords** The Ottoman Empire · The law · Judicial decision · Behaviors · Changing rules

This chapter focuses on the rule of law concept in a historical context. To achieve this goal, we take the rule of law as an institution that was able



B. Altay and F. Oğuz, *Rules, Contracts and Law Enforcement in the Ottoman Empire*, Palgrave Studies in Institutions, Economics and Law, https://doi.org/10.1007/978-3-030-79577-1_3

to limit the coercive power of the states. As it is given above, the states mostly relied on taxation to provide financial resources for increasing needs due to the exogenous factors and endogenous dynamics during the pre-industrial period. An important example is found in the fiscal history of the Ottoman Empire. In contrast to the classical age (1300–1600), state finance is surrounded by tax-farming contracts, in which the state delegated authority to agents from different groups. Nevertheless, tax-farming contracts have destructive effects on the long-term stability of fiscal revenues. Mainstream Ottoman historians examine these effects within the institutional structure by focusing on limited contract durations, corrupt and venal incentives of the agents, and confiscatory behaviors of the sultans. The recent literature, however, overlooks the place of Ottoman rulers regarding the law.

During the pre-industrial period, one of the most important obstacles within the contractual relations was that the state as principal was above the law in the Ottoman Empire. The same existed in Western European societies. The state's commitment became questionable, and its ability to find financial resources should be weaker than wealthier groups in the society. In this sense, the state's power was related to the sultan's cultivation of its agents—both state and non-state agents. The state took these agents as their financiers to support increasing financial needs and political apparatus. In the case of the Ottoman Empire, however, these agents consisted of powerful groups, who were granted a title by the authority of the state. Similar coalitions, on the other hand, emerged between the rulers and hereditary families, who inherited their title from their families. This allowed these powerful families to establish coalitions with each other through intermarriages (Root, 1989, p. 242). The Ottoman state deteriorated possible coalitions among its agents by granting titles with its coercive power. One of the most important deficiencies of the recent literature was to accept the coercive power of the state by focusing on its ability to grant titles. The contractual relations, however, provided another equilibrium through the tax-farming institution in the rule of law context. Yet, these arguments did not mean that the Ottoman state had absolute power or no power over contractual relations (see Chapter 7).

There is growing literature over the rule of law and economic performances in a historical context (see, for example, Acemoglu & Robinson, 2012; North et al., 2009; Tilly, 1990; van Zanden, 2009). To limit the boundaries of this book, we choose to focus on the NWW perspective in examining the rule of law in the Ottoman Empire. Although the recent literature has taken the structure of law as given, this book interprets the structure of law and its rules as a part of equilibrium that emerged from interactions among institutions, players, beliefs, and behavior (Hadfield & Weingast, 2014, p. 23). In other words, the structure of the law is considered as a dynamic process that moved from one equilibrium to another in changing institutional structures of the Ottoman Empire.

State structures as political institutions are crucial to determine the strategies of the rulers in both contractual relations and judicial decisions. The costs of revenue extracting and borrowing depend on these non-economic institutions. As it is argued by Charles Tilly (1990), Europe consisted of fragmented states, except France and England, like city-states and feudal states and small principalities until the nineteenth century. The fragmented political structures direct rulers to a dilemma due to the increasing political and military competition among each other. The dilemma emerges from not only increasing needs for financial resources in the short term but also sustaining social and political order without violence.

In the rule of law context and among various ranges of literature, this book includes novel perspectives given in *Social Order and Violence* by North et al. (2009). The perspective reflects the relationship between the political structures and the law in a historical context. Furthermore, this perspective provides tools to understand the choices and preferences of central authorities as well as doorstep conditions of the rule of law regarding judicial decisions. The theoretical framework of the NWW approach is based on private property rights. It is well known that the dominant mechanism was to sustain state ownership in allocating contracts through auction mechanism.

Although the Ottoman Empire refrained from promoting private ownership on financial resources, usufruct rights had been one of the most important mechanisms in contractual relations. As given above in detail, the intended duration of contracts determined the period of usufruct rights within the institutional structure. The confiscatory behavior of the central authority caused to emerge a commitment problem on the usufruct rights of the agents. While the state ownership provided a power to the central authority in allocating contracts, the agents expected their contracts to continue as long as they received their usufruct rights. The State ownership was the main outcome of the traditional structure of the Ottoman Empire. However, well-defined property rights were still the main determinant in the emergence of effective economic results and strategies of agents. As expected, agents would engage in productive economic activities as long as their property rights were protected. Within the scope of this study, the main actors should be the legal structure in limiting the power of the central authority. Although courts and judges were commonly used within the economic exchanges, the state control was limited to the judgments on the opportunistic behavior of the central authority. The historical evidence showed that agents failed to establish a cooperative body against Sharia courts and the central authority. The proposed reasons given above made the framework based on NWW approach compatible with the case of tax-farming contracts. From this point, one should assume that each contracting relation given in this study will be based on state ownership.

Daron Acemoglu and James A. Robinson (2012) discuss political structures regarding two different institutional structures. They examine the institutional structures of different societies with similar non-economic institutions, including cultural beliefs, traditions, and cognations. The political institutions, however, are the main determinant of which economic institutions would surround the economic environment of societies in the historical context. The societies with inclusive institutions have better economic performances rather than those with extractive institutions. The reason behind this argument is that inclusive institutions entailed higher participation in economic activities from different groups of societies. The extractive institutions, on the other hand, direct political actors to create monopoly power over economic institutions or to promote mechanisms to protect their economic interests. Acemoglu and Robinson (2012, p. 77) argue that technology and education are the main conditions to change the institutional structure from extractive to inclusive. In this sense, the new technologies cause creative destruction over the extractive institutions, and they encourage well-defined property rights, enforceable contracts, and free entry to the new business.

Charles Tilly (1990) argues the institutional structure through political structures under capital-intense and coercion-intense state structures, particularly during the sixteenth and the seventeenth centuries. This perspective presents the effects of small institutional differences over the economic performances, focusing on centralized and decentralized structures of different societies, including the Ottoman Empire and European states. The main deficiency is that there is a lack of explanation over the transition from coercion-intense structures to capital-intense structures.

The NWW approach, however, allows establishing a deeper analysis of how some societies achieved to establish the rule of law and others did not. In a historical context, this approach provides more tools through doorstep conditions. These conditions are also related to contractual relations and judicial decisions, including pre-industrial period societies. More importantly, the doorstep conditions of this approach are compatible with the political and economic institutions of the Ottoman Empire. Before examining the concept of the rule of law in the Ottoman Empire, it would be useful to briefly dwell on the environment in which the state structure emerged.

The Ottomans were a small principality (*beylik*) in the South Thrace of North-Western Anatolia in the first years of the fourteenth century. The Anatolia and Balkan territories consisted of small-scale feudal states and small principalities except for Byzantine Empire in Istanbul. The fragmented structure of these territories was supposed to create a competitive structure among these small-scale political organizations. This happened until the middle of the fifteenth century. The Ottomans developed better military organizations and political mechanisms to dominate other small-scale political organizations. The conquest of Istanbul in 1453 allowed the Ottomans to establish a large-scale political organization in an empire context. During the same period, the Ottoman Empire also achieved to establish an integrated and bureaucratized political structure in its territories (Abou-El-Haj, 2000, pp. 37–39; Karaman, 2009, p. 691).

The sixteenth century was the period when the Ottoman military and political powers peaked with an integrated and bureaucratized structure. During the same periods, the fragmented structure of Europe still existed. European states had to deal with organizing economic and political institutions in limited territories (Abou-El-Haj, 2000, p. 29; Tilly, 1990). The Ottoman Empire, on the other side, faced different institutional constraints due to the rapid territorial expansion and larger territories. The territorial expansion caused endogenous problems in controlling lands and sustaining political order. To solve these problems, the central authority had to choose between land-holding aristocracy and military-based agents. In other words, the struggle between hereditary families and high-ranking military-based agents determined the institutional environment of the Ottoman Empire.

During the competition among these powerful groups, the central authority supported the high-ranking military/administrative-based agents (*Kul system*) as well as judicial/religious-based agents for various reasons. The first was related to the economic power of land-holding aristocracy to organize military power against the central authority. The second was that the Ottoman rulers employed these agents in the provinces they conquered. They guaranteed security for properties of local people through the agents. Thus, the political institution was surrounded by status groups instead of feudal lords, elites, or barons as in Old Regime France. Employing agents made it difficult to invade territories. It was easy to subvert elites in Europe by offering them higher economic and political privileges, and elites could create rebellion (Inalcık, 2017, pp. 227–229).

Delegating authority to military/administrative-based and judicial/religious-based agents was directly related to the structure of law in the Ottoman Empire. Max Weber (1954) defined the political and legal structure of the Ottoman Empire as "sultanism" (See, also, Inalcık, 2017, 2018). The main characteristic of this political organization was based on traditions. In other words, the Ottoman rulers were legitimate if they preserved the traditional structure of the empire. The Weber approach called as "sultanism" directed Ottoman rulers to employ different groups of agents instead of land-holding aristocracy to exercise their power in territories. We differ from the Weber thesis on "sultanism" and offer an alternative with a systematic analysis following contractual relations and law enforcement (see, Chapter 7).

*Kanun* was the main legal structure that organized the responsibilities of agents and determining constraints of bureaucratic apparatus within the institutional structure. As an Islamic society and the Turkish dynasty, the Ottoman Empire combined two separate legal traditions. It asserted the independence of state affairs and public law by implementing Urfi Law and Sharia Law at the same time (Inalcık, 2018, p. 264). Through these laws, Ottoman rulers achieved cooperation with the Muslim judiciary and clergy. Furthermore, the structure of law allowed jurists to enforce the rules of Hanafi School. This decision directly affected the direction of the economic performances by allowing the central authority to intervene in rules to cope with arising economic problems. From the beginning of the classical age, the Ottoman rulers prevented judicial/religious-based agents from enforcing *urfi* law, and they enforced these laws independently from Sharia law (Inalcık, 2017, p. 65). The monopoly power of Ottoman rulers over political and religious decisions deteriorated from the beginning of the seventeenth century. Judicial/religious-based agents establish coalitions with other traditional groups within the tax-farming institutions, and they increased their role in state affairs during the pre-industrial period. Thus, the relationship between the legal structure and contracts became crucial in determining the economic performance of the Ottoman Empire in the pre-industrial period.

The NWW perspective provides an explanation of the political and legal process on the relationship between the economic performance and the structure of law, including the rule of law. This perspective mainly argued three different social orders on the way of establishing the rule of law: *natural state*, *limited access order*, and *open access order* (North et al., 2009, pp. 18–25). The main characteristics of these orders were to reduce violence and allocate financial resources toward productive areas. The first social order, *the natural state*, represented both small social groups as hunter-gatherer societies and earlier forms of state organizations for about ten millennia (North et al., 2009, p. 2).

In terms of the rule of law, the political and economic relations were based on personal relationships among powerful individuals within the society. The economic and political privileges were shared among powerful groups within dominant coalitions. More importantly, these groups prevented other individuals from entering coalitions. In other words, powerful groups had strong incentives to protect their economic and political interests through personal relationships. In these societies, powerful groups had incentives to protect their privileges and interests. They collectively resisted the changes that might disturb their gains. Violence could stay at low levels under the natural states through personal relationships among powerful groups.

*Limited access order*, however, includes more complex political and legal structures regarding the former social order. The state became one of the most important parts of coalitions. Powerful groups had to establish coalitions with the state if they needed to maintain their economic and political privileges. The courts were another important non-economic institution that emerged under the limited access order. The elites' incentives on maintaining coalitions continued as a dominant strategy. The courts and the law enforcement became crucial tools of the states in protecting the interests and privileges of coalitions. Even if the law and formal rules emerged within the institutional environment, these were enforced for specific aims of coalitions. *Open access order* had three different mechanisms: (1) consolidated organization of military and police forces is subject to the control of the political system; (2) the political system must be constrained by a set of institutions and incentives that limit the illegitimate use of violence; 3) for a political faction or party to remain in power (North et al., 2009, p. 22). These three elements are crucial to limit the monopoly power of coalitions. Imposing constraints on coalitions, the political structure would be open to political and economic entries for each group that existed in society. Furthermore, the open entry in economic and political domains promoted impersonal relations among players.

The higher participation in political and economic processes provides credible incentives for competitive structure. The competition among different groups in varied ranges decreased the possibility of illegitimate uses of violence. North et al. (2009, p. 23). defined impersonality as treating every single individual the same. Furthermore, impersonality promoted *perpetually lived organizations*. The existence of such organizations was independent of their members or founders. The competitive structure and perpetually lived organizations changed the economic structure by promoting creative destruction. The innovation entailed productivity over financial resources and exploitation of new resources. Thus, the rent-seeking activities could be abandoned in favor of profit-seeking activities under the open access order. North et al. (2009, p. 26) argued that societies could transform their social order even if they achieved the following doorstep conditions: (1) Rule of law for elites; (2) Perpetually lived forms of public and private elite organizations, including the highest political institution—the state; (3) Consolidated political control of the military.

The Ottoman Empire was a representative of limited access order as other European societies during the pre-industrial period. The state established coalitions with powerful groups through contractual relations. Contrary to European societies, Ottoman rulers eliminated land-holding aristocracy, elites, and feudal lords, and they chose to support powerful groups (Karaman, 2009; Karaman & Pamuk, 2010; Pamuk, 2004). Each powerful group was a member of status groups. The status group meant that the titles were granted by the Ottoman rulers. The main purpose of the rulers was to maintain the balance of power among different socio-economic groups. The competition that was created by the hands of rulers directed status groups to concentrate on keeping their interests within the balance. The Ottoman rulers prevented one group from dominating others. Contractual relations were the main tool for this purpose. Furthermore, the state established a multilateral monitoring mechanism. Judicial/religious-based agents had the authority to monitor military/administrative-based agents through courts. The latter group was an important part of law enforcement. If the balance was maintained, the state could keep violence at low rates. What the state made differently was dividing the law into two parts. The traditional law (Urfi law) provided tools for the state to intervene in judicial decisions. The sharia law (religious law) allowed judicial/religious-based agents to keep their interests. The rulers also employed *janissary* corps to limit the power of military/administrative-based agents, who were able to make contractual arrangements. Tax-farming contracts provided political and economic interests for these groups. Even if the state imposed a multilateral monitoring mechanism to limit the power of status groups, there were not only economic and political privileges but also legal privileges.

In this sense, the doorstep conditions of the NWW approach emerged in the Ottoman Empire during the pre-industrial period. The state promoted the rule of law for powerful status groups (Kuran & Rubin, 2018). Tax-farming contracts were perpetually lived institutions as well as Sharia courts and traditional law (Urfi law). Finally, the state always kept a consolidated central army to keep the balance between political actors within the institutional environment. The problem was why the Ottoman Empire failed to establish the rule of law even if the doorstep conditions existed.

Why did the institutional structure fail to promote impersonal intra-status group relationships? Why did status groups fail to recognize impersonal exchanges that would increase their interest in the long term? If the substantial proportion of the rule of law literature took the structure of law as given, it would be difficult to find out the complete answers to such questions. Gillian K. Hadfield and Weingast (2014, p. 30) argued that microfoundations of the behaviors affected and generated diverse legal orders in societies. It was important to identify institutions that promoted independent judicial decisions and behaviors. Because the states were willing to impose efficient legal structures, there were always powerful groups to sabotage institutional change or to resist changes that deteriorated their self-interests (Acemoglu & Robinson, 2012). In this sense, behaviors and beliefs had a substantial influence on producing aggregate outcomes. Except for Hadfield and Weingast, a substantial part of the literature overlooked how preconditions came into existence and were sustained (Hadfield & Weingast, 2014, p. 31).

The following chapters examine the evolutionary process of the legal structure by focusing on behaviors of status groups within the institutional environment. The legal order is an equilibrium that emerged from choices players. The question is what was the process by which legal order dominated the other in the Ottoman Empire, and what was the aggregate outcome on the way to the rule of law and economic performance in the long term? The following chapters provide information about players' decisions and behaviors through tax-farming contracts. We use tax-farming contracts because of their nature, including the choices and behaviors of the players. These contracts reflect coordination problems within the institutional environment. Furthermore, they are important tools because the contract market surrounded more than half of the financial resources of the state.

## References

Abou-El-Haj, R. A. (2000). *Modern Devletin Doğası: 16. yüzyıldan 18. yüzyıla Osmanlı İmparatorluğu* (O. Özel, Trans.). Imge Kitabevi.

Acemoglu, D., & Robinson, J. A. (2012). *Why nations fail? The origins of power, prosperity and poverty*. Profile Books.

Hadfield, G. K., & Weingast, B. R. (2014). Microfoundations of the rule of law. *Annual Review of Political Science, 17*, 21–42.

İnalcık, H. (2017). *The Ottoman Empire and Europe*. Kronik.

İnalcık, H. (2018). *The Ottoman Empire: Sultan, society and economy*. Kronik.

Karaman, K. (2009). Decentralized coercion and self-restraint in provincial taxation: The Ottoman Empire, 15th–16th centuries. *Journal of Economic Behavior & Organization, 71*(3), 690–703.

Karaman, K. K., & Pamuk, Ş. (2010). Ottoman state finances in European perspective. *The Journal of Economic History, 70*(3), 593–629.

Kuran, T., & Rubin, J. (2018). The financial power of the powerless: Interest rates and socioeconomic status under partial rule of law. *Economic Journal, 128*(609), 758–796.

North, D. C., Wallis, J. J., & Weingast, B. R. (2009). *Violence and social orders: A conceptual framework for interpreting recorded human history*. Cambridge University Press.

Pamuk, Ş. (2004). Institutional change and the longevity of the Ottoman Empire, 1500–1800. *The Journal of Interdisciplinary History, 35*(2), 225–247.

Root, H. L. (1989). Tying the king's hands: Credible commitment and royal fiscal policy during the old regime. *Rationality and Society, 1*(2), 240–258.

Tilly, C. (1990). *Coercion, capital and European states, AD 990–1992*. Princeton University Press.

Van Zanden, J. L. (2009). *The long road to the industrial revolution, the European economy in a global perspective, 1000–1800*. E. J. Brill.

Weber, M. (1954). *On law in economy and society* (E. Shils & M. Rheinstein, Trans.). Harvard University Press.

CHAPTER 4

# Place of Tax-Farming Institutions in the Ottoman Economy

**Abstract** This chapter focuses certainly on economic indicators to examine the economic performance of the Ottoman Empire during the pre-industrial period. Despite the lack of data for developing economies before industrialization, tax revenues provide sufficient information to understand long-term economic performances. The estimates made by Maddison Project provide other economic data based on per capita GDP levels of the Ottoman Empire, from the beginning of the sixteenth century to the nineteenth century. The historical evidence shows that the tax-farming institutions surrounded a substantial part of tax revenues in the Ottoman Empire. The efficiency of these institutions determines the level of tax revenues. Their effectiveness allows a comparative analysis of the institutions of societies through per capita tax revenues.

**Keywords** The Ottoman Empire · Economic performances · Pre-industrial period · Tax revenues · Per capita GDP

The Ottomans[1] established coalitions through tax-farming contracts since its early years. The tax-farming institutions emerged in different

[1] We chose to use the term "Ottomans" until the conquest of Istanbul.



B. Altay and F. Oğuz, *Rules, Contracts and Law Enforcement in the Ottoman Empire*, Palgrave Studies in Institutions, Economics and Law, https://doi.org/10.1007/978-3-030-79577-1_4

forms depending on the economic and political conditions of the times. Endogenous and exogenous factors played major roles in the way tax-farming contracts are designed and implemented.

Industrialization caused changes in political structures in European societies as well as the Ottoman Empire toward centralization. Until this period, decentralized institutions surrounded both the economic and political environments of "Powers" between 1500 and 1800 (Rubin, 2017; van Zanden, 2009). The recent literature argued that the Ottoman Empire was one of the most important "Powers" during the early modern period (Hoffman, 2015; Kennedy, 1988; Tilly, 1990). The term "Power" was used for states which hold military power to change the balance of power. The Ottoman state established its institutional structure to promote not only economic and political order but also military power. The military-based agents surrounded most of the institutional environment through state offices. The Ottoman Empire did not establish a new kind of institutional structure in organizing contractual relations between the central authority and its agents. Instead, the timar institution was reformed as an innovative design from earlier institutions of both the Byzantine Empire and the Seljuk Dynasty (Tabakoğlu, 2008). The new institution which was based on negotiations and bargains dominated the economic environment until the end of the sixteenth century (Tezcan, 2010; Yaycioglu, 2016). The Ottoman rulers needed contractual relations with agents to sustain legitimacy, political order, and financial resources. The pragmatic and flexible structure of the empire allowed the central authority to change its institutional structures to preserve legitimacy and financial resources. The structure of the law and judicial/religious-based agents played a crucial role particularly on legitimacy in contractual relations (Rubin, 2017).

The timar institution was used in the allocation of certain economic units toward powerful groups. The central authority established coalitions with different groups until the last decades of the fifteenth century. There were different reasons for employing diverse powerful groups within the institutional environment. First, the Ottoman rulers needed the economic and military support of powerful groups in conquered territories. The centralization was weak to sustain legitimacy and political order. The military struggle with Timur's Mongol Empire aided the fragmentation of the Ottomans at the beginning of the fifteenth century. Even if the Ottomans achieved to establish integrated economic and political structure during the same century, this directed Ottoman rulers to change the institutional structure as well as contracting parties. Second, contracting parties mainly consisted of two diverse powerful groups. The first group consisted of settled elites who had the authority over provinces. The land-holding aristocracy had its economic power as well as military power within the institutional environment. The second group included military-based agents emerging from the *Kul system* or *devshirme*. Contrary to land-holding aristocracy, the Ottoman rulers granted titles and economic sources to this group of agents. These agents had limited economic and military capacity compared with the first group. The authority of the second group bounded with the limits of the right granted by the central authority. The conquest of Istanbul changed the state structure, and hence, the Ottomans became an empire.

The transformation of the state structure to administrative/military-based agents increased competition among powerful groups. Competition emerged as a struggle between the land-holding aristocracy and administrative/military-based agents. During the reign of Mehmed II, covering the last decades of the fifteenth century, the balance of power shifted on behalf of administrative/military-based agents (Pamuk, 2004a, p. 234). Mehmed II chose to support its agents under the ***kul system*** against the land-holding aristocracy. The power of powerful groups was bound to their titles that were granted by Ottoman rulers. In other words, Ottoman rulers limited the power of their agents. This limitation over the reign of powerful groups was based not only on political matters but also on economic status within the institutional environment. Contrary to land-holding aristocracy, agents had limited financial resources to innovate and develop mechanisms limiting the absolute power of the central authority. As Kıvanç Karaman (2009, p. 691) argued, the classical age (1453–1600) is the period of self-restraint in provincial taxation, centralization in the political structure, and systematization and codification in the legal structure.

The Ottoman Empire achieved a rapid territorial expansion from the fifteenth century. This expansion was the primary outcome of the institutional structure rather than military superiority. The timar institution dominated not only the military organization but also economic, political, and legal structure. The entire economy of the empire was based on negotiations and bargaining through timar contracts.

The elimination of land-holding aristocracy paved the way for two main groups. The first group consisted of administrative/military-based agents granted a title by the central authority. The second group emerged as pillars of the check and balance system over the actions of the first groups. Judicial/religious-based agents, in this sense, executed two main functions in favor of the central authority. The first was to maintain traditions, and the second was to practice law through courts (Chapter 5). These groups generated *Askeri* class, who were exempt from tax. The taxpayers consisted of larger groups, including farmers, manufacturers, merchants, and workers, called *Reaya* class. The central authority gave particular importance to maintain the balance between different groups within *Askeri* class (İnalcık, 2018, p. 133). As it was given in Chapter 5, the competition among powerful groups (economic, military, and judicial agents) was one of the most important determinants of why the rule of law failed to emerge during the early modern period.

The timar institution, however, surrounded the economic environment of the Ottoman Empire. This institution and its mechanisms were based on agency relations. The central authority allocated economic units (tax collecting rights of agricultural lands, entire villages, mines, etc.) and financial resources (customs, direct taxes, etc.) toward its agents called *sipahi*. These groups consisted of elite infantries in the Ottoman army. The abandonment of land-holding aristocracy paved the way for these groups of agents considered administrative/military-based agents from the last decades of the fifteenth century. Contrary to aristocracy, a *sipahi* granted his title by the central authority through timar contracts. The emergence of coalitions, unlike European societies, did not emerge through state offices. The administrative/military-based agents had limited authority to implement the rules of the central authority. Courts and the highest judges (*kadi*) were the main representative bodies of the central authority (Chapter 5). The administrative/military-based agents executed different functions mostly related to economic and military organizations. Under the institutional structure, the central authority employed these groups of agents to reduce its transaction costs like security, production, and tax-collecting (Barkan, 1980, pp. 286–287). Each agent got a part of the economic unit from the central authority. The allocation of timar contracts was based on a merit system. The beneficial agents during campaigns had the right to obtain a timar contract from the central authority. Each agent held these rights on land for the duration of their duty. There were two main expectations from agents. Their first duty was to collect taxes for the central budget. The secondary duty was to train new troops for the army. The economic scale of contracts forced agents to train more *cebelü* (military units raised by administrative/military-based agents).

The administrative/military-based agents with contracts had different forms according to their economic returns: *timar*, *zeamet*, and *hâs* (Darling, 1996, p. 25). Each form was determined regarding the gains from economic units. *Timar*[2] was the lowest level sub-contract. Administrative/military-based agents, who were beneficial during campaigns, had the right to obtain this form of sub-contracts. The annual revenue of a *timar* contract was up to 20.000 akches within the institutional environment. Each agent was responsible for training soldiers one *cebelü* per 3.000 akches. One agent holding a *timar* contract with 18.000 akches gains, for instance, had to raise six *cebelü* for the military. Agents could increase the gains of their economic units by organizing production and creating incentive mechanisms for taxpayers. If the gains from the economic unit exceeded 20.000 akches, the central authority had the right to change the form of the contract. The second sub-contract, in this sense, was *Zeamet*. The economic gains of this contract were between 20.000 akche and 100.000 akche. *Zeamet* contracts were mostly obtained by experienced administrative/military-based agents and high-ranking bureaucracy. One rough estimate argued that there were 38.259 *timar* contracts and 2.375 *zeamet* contracts during the sixteenth century, and these numbers raised to 78.675 timar contracts and 4.877 zeamet contracts in the following century (Afyoncu, İslam Ansiklopedisi, p. 163). The last sub-contract is called *hâs* with an income of more than 100.000 akche. The central authority, including relatives of sultans, viziers, governors, had the economic and political power to obtain *hâs* contracts. Ömer Lütfi Barkan (1980, p. 807) showed that almost 88% of state revenues were under contractual relations in 1527/28.

The central authority directed the costs of certain transactions to agents by allocating these contracts under certain terms. First, military/administrative-based agents were responsible for securing their economic units. The central budget was not obliged to reserve a share for law enforcers. Furthermore, the central authority had the chance to eliminate intermediaries in tax-collecting. The agents collected taxes in kind. Transferring tax revenues in kind was a costly transaction. The agents were also responsible for converting revenues in kind into cash (Genç,

[2] The timar institution and timar contracts represent the institutional structure. *Timar*, written in italic, means a specific form of timar contracts.

**Table 4.1** The state finance in comparative perspective, 1500–1800

| *Years* | *England* | *France* | *Spain* | *Venice* | *Austria* | *Russia* | *Prussia* | *Ottomans* |
|---|---|---|---|---|---|---|---|---|
| *Budget revenues (Tons of Silver, Ottomans 1500 = 100)* | | | | | | | | |
| 1500/49 | 16 | 67 | 39 | 34 | | | | 100 |
| 1550/99 | 28 | 117 | 83 | 38 | | | | 117 |
| 1600/49 | 51 | 227 | 332 | 52 | | | 3 | 76 |
| 1650/99 | 151 | 812 | 318 | 52 | 58 | | 5 | 104 |
| 1700/49 | 431 | 677 | 169 | 73 | 159 | 69 | 34 | 132 |
| 1750/99 | 633 | 834 | 339 | 64 | 269 | 212 | 156 | 113 |
| *Per capita tax revenues (in grams of Silver, Ottomans 1500 = 100)* | | | | | | | | |
| 1500/49 | 73 | 95 | 171 | 367 | | | | 100 |
| 1550/99 | 119 | 145 | 255 | 395 | | | | 104 |
| 1600/49 | 203 | 242 | 834 | 501 | | | 32 | 63 |
| 1650/99 | 516 | 754 | 763 | 567 | 141 | | 119 | 89 |
| 1700/49 | 1226 | 580 | 381 | 618 | 208 | 83 | 328 | 113 |
| 1750/99 | 1455 | 650 | 616 | 483 | 307 | 199 | 709 | 95 |

*Notes* These data are derived from various sources and reflect approximate values. See, Genç and Özvar (2006), Karaman and Pamuk (2013), Brandt et al. (2014), and Ma and Rubin (2019)

2000, p. 101). Each agent had the right to deduct a share of their expenditures from tax revenues. The remaining share was the state revenue. Contractual relations allowed the central authority to reduce costs of tax collection, produce certain public goods and keep a regular army.

Table 4.1 presents a comparison of state revenues and per capita tax revenues for the early modern period. For each society, central authorities employed similar revenue extracting institutions with different mechanisms. Formal and informal rules that emerged in societies entailed institutional diversity. The institutional structure, however, is based on contractual relations between the central authorities and powerful groups. Central authorities mostly preferred to allocate tax-collecting rights through auction mechanisms. Once a contract was established between contracting parties, how the game was played determined the way of economic performances in the long term. The first two sub-periods represented the century when the timar institution dominated the institutional environment in the Ottoman Empire. For several reasons given in historical background, the Ottoman Empire had better performance compared to European societies in budget revenues. On the other side, European societies had slightly better performance in terms of per capita revenues during the same period. This reverse data might emerge from two different reasons. First, the Ottoman Empire population was higher than European societies. Secondly, and more importantly, rapid territorial expansion provided financial resources in addition to revenues from tax-farming institutions.

The territorial expansion of the Ottoman Empire continued during the seventeenth century. The seventeenth-century expansion was slower compared to the sixteenth century. Slowing territorial expansion deteriorated state revenues. The emergence of exogenous shocks and changing the perception of agents forced the central authority to change the institutional structure. The monetary-based contractual relations caused changes in the rules of the game. The abandonment of the timar institution in favor of tax-farming institutions reversed inefficient outcomes relative to the previous century. Recent literature argued that the Ottoman tax collection performances paled compared to European societies (Ma & Rubin, 2019, p. 287). The Ottoman Empire collected from 1/5 to 1/10 of the per capita taxes of the European States—England, France, Spain, and Venice. These rates continued to increase during the eighteenth century, while the central authority changed the rules of the game by imposing lifetime tax-farming contracts.

The classical age surrounded by the timar institution allowed the Ottoman Empire to rapidly expand its territories during the sixteenth century. The central authority achieved to finance a large army without using substantial resources from the state revenues. The Ottoman Empire had higher tax revenues compared to other "Powers", particularly during the sixteenth century. The higher revenues emerged not only from efficient contractual relations but also soils of wars during this period. In terms of per capita tax revenues, the premium was close to the European societies. The larger territories entailed higher transaction costs compared to other "Powers". Contrary to feudal lords and elites of European societies, military/administrative-based agents had no authority to determine tax rates within the institutional structure. Instead, the Ottoman Empire imposed a low tax rate with its higher centralized and integrated structure compared to Europe (Karaman, 2009, p. 691).

The seventeenth century was a period of transformations in economic, political, and institutional structures. These transformations had two main sources: exogenous shocks and endogenous dynamics. The capital inflow from the New World and changing military technology were the main exogenous shocks that forced the Ottoman Empire to change its institutional structure from the last decades of the sixteenth century

(Tezcan, 2010). The most important outcome emerged in the allocation of contracts within the timar institution. The growth rate of territorial expansion started to slow down from the last decades of the sixteenth century. The military technology and its superiority became insufficient to overcome the well-equipped regular armies of European societies. In terms of modern economics, the contract market faced a shortage problem following diminishes in military superiority compared to European societies. The supply of timar contracts lagged the increasing demand for timar contracts by administrative/military-based agents. Granting titles was the dominant strategy of the central authority to sustain economic and political order. Agents directed their interests to be members of administrative/military-based agents or judicial/religious-based agents to enjoy higher economic returns under the domination of the timar institution. If the Ottoman Empire enhanced its territories, the demand for titles and timar contracts grew in substantial proportions. When Ottoman expansion reached its natural limits, the shortage problem entailed changes in the perception of agents, and hence, exogenous shocks entailed changes in endogenous dynamics within the institutional environment.

The first outcome of exogenous shocks was devaluations in Ottoman currencies (Pamuk, 2000). The central authority decreased the silver content of *akche* from the last decades of the sixteenth century. This directed administrative/military-based agents to crop higher shares from tax revenues to finance their increasing costs. Secondly, administrative/military-based agents suffered from other costs due to the long-duration and long-distance campaigns. When the shortage emerged in the contract market, the central authority chose to allocate new timar contracts from different regions that were far from Western Anatolia and Balkan territories. Thus, the administrative/military-based agents abstained from military campaigns that caused a diminution in the military superiority of the Ottoman Empire. Thirdly, and more importantly, administrative/military-based agents started to direct their financial resources to obtain contracts by the by-passing merit system. Directing financial resources to obtain contracts instead of participating in campaigns became the dominant strategy due to its lower risks. In the shadow of exogenous shocks, the Ottoman Empire faced two main problems: violence and low financial resources. The *Jalali Revolts*, driven

**Table 4.2** Ottoman economy in global perspective: per capita GDP levels, 1500–1820

| | | | | |
|---|---|---|---|---|
| *Absolute values* | | | | |
| 1500 | 1650 | 1700 | 1750 | 1820 |
| 600 | 600 | 632 | 648 | 740 |
| *Relative values* (World = 100) | | | | |
| 106 | 101 | 103 | 105 | 111 |
| *Relative values (Europe = 100)* | | | | |
| 78 | 68 | 64 | 65 | 62 |
| *Relative values (Middle East = 100)* | | | | |
| 102 | 102 | 107 | 113 | 122 |
| *Relative values (Asia = 100)* | | | | |
| 106 | 105 | 110 | 113 | 127 |

*Source* Maddison (2001, 2003)

mostly by military-based groups, deteriorated not only the military organization but also agricultural production during the first half of the seventeenth century (Barkey, 1994; Darling, 1996, p. 23).

The reflection of endogenous factors was decreasing per capita tax revenues during the seventeenth century (see Table 4.1). The most important but least noticeable result of these riots was the changes in the structure and dominance of the agents in which military-based agents were surpassed by judicial/religious-based agents and provincial notables (non-state agents) with different titles from the seventeenth century (Rubin, 2017). Even if administrative/military-based agents existed within the institutional environment, their wealth reversed and lagged the wealth of other groups of agents until the nineteenth century.

The central authority mitigated increasing costs of violence and opportunistic behavior agents by changing its institutional structure called the tax-farming (*iltizam*) institution from the last decades of the sixteenth century. The main purpose of the central authority was to increase its financial resources in the short term and sustain political order within the territories. The tax-farming institution was also based on contractual relations. In terms of per capita GDP, the small institutional differences, however, entailed economic divergence from European societies from the beginning of the seventeenth century (see Table 4.2).

The economic history literature over economic performances of societies argued that the divergence started before industrialization. Long-term estimates of per capita incomes show divergence, particularly between European societies and other societies. Small institutional differences were the main source of the divergence. Table 4.2 presents a comparison based on per capita GDP levels from the sixteenth century to the nineteenth century. This table suggests that per capita GDP levels of European societies and the Ottoman Empire were close to each other in the 1500s. The per capita GDP level of the Ottoman Empire is 78% of Europe. This rate has a decreasing trend toward the eighteenth century, the period when exogenous shocks and endogenous dynamics forced central authorities to change institutional structures. In the period between the first and second years, the data shows that the per capita GDP level of the Ottoman Empire stayed at the same level. Although per capita GDP remains at the same level, this is high compared to the average level of the World, Asia, and the Middle East. However, the per capita GDP of the Ottoman Empire decreased 68% of the European average until the middle of the seventeenth century.

Since the eighteenth century, the per capita GDP levels of the Ottoman Empire have slightly increased in time. The increases in per capita GDP levels have caused divergence compared to average levels of the World, Asia, and the Middle East. This shows that the Ottoman Empire had better economic performance regarding the substantial part of the World, except Europe. Meanwhile, the divergence has increased between Europe and the periphery starting from the Ottoman Empire towards Asia. Europe has achieved to increase in per capita GDP levels during the eighteenth century. The disparity in per capita GDP levels seems so important that Europe has doubled its levels compared to Asia and the Middle East. The period presented in Table 4.2 is unable to include effects of industrialization that emerged in Europe. The economic history literature argues that a substantial part of Europe, except England, achieved to adopt productive and effective mechanisms of industrialization during the nineteenth century. The economic effects of industrialization, in this sense, should emerge in European economies following the age of revolutions, from the second half of the nineteenth century. Thus, fiscal capacity and revenue extracting mechanisms should be incorporated into the center of economic analysis.

Table 4.2 presents per capita GDP levels of the Ottoman Empire in the long-term perspective. The data used in Table 4.2 shows rough estimates based on 1990 Geary-Khamis US Dollars. Although these findings have deficiencies to indicate absolute per capita GDP levels of both the Ottoman Empire and other societies, these comparative estimates and other attempts are the only sources to examine long-term economic performance of the Ottoman Empire. The data suggests that the Ottoman Empire achieved a modest economic growth from the beginning of the sixteenth century to the first decades of the nineteenth century. More importantly, the economic growth stays almost at the same level until the middle of the eighteenth century. As it can be seen, the economic performance of the Ottoman Empire was above the world average in a comparative perspective (Pamuk, 2018). This situation is valid compared to Middle East and Asia economies. However, the data also suggests relative backwardness of the Ottoman Empire regarding European economies during the same period. This study tries to explain this divergence through contract relations, law, and the practices of Ottoman *Urfi Law*. It is shown that although the Ottoman Empire employed and developed similar institutional mechanisms with European societies, non-economic institutions played a crucial role in creating small differences in the rules of the game. Thus, the divergence emerges in not only industrialization but also early modern period. Even if the recent literature estimates higher per capita GDP levels for the Ottoman Empire, the gap between European societies continues and the divergence exists until the First World War (Bolt & Van Zanden, 2014; Broadberry & Klein, 2012; Bulut & Altay, 2021).

The central authority delegated agents in tax collecting by allocating tax-farming contracts. Instead of a merit system, an auction mechanism determined the price of contracts that were committed by the agents (*mültezims,* non-state agents) in contractual relations (Çizakça, 1996, p. 140; Darling, 1996, p. 119; Salzmann, 2004, p. 113). In other words, each agent offered a price, and central authority delegated the highest bidder as an agent in state offices. The main purpose was to direct the financial resources of agents toward the central budget. The central authority noticed opportunistic behaviors of administrative/military-based agents in capturing timar contracts. The merit system left its place to collusion between judicial/religious-based agents and administrative/military-based agents within the timar institution. Judicial groups used their authority to allocate timar contracts by bypassing the merit system. The rent emerged within the collusion shared among powerful groups. Thus, the institutional change emerged to direct these rents toward the central budget within the institutional environment.

The central authority, however, gave up enforcing participating campaign rules on agents within the new contractual arrangement. The deterioration of the merit system was not the only reason behind the institutional change. The changing military technology forced the Ottoman Empire to change its military organizations. The war against the Habsburg Empire showed that the military organization of the Ottoman Empire started to lose its efficiency compared to European foes (Karaman & Pamuk, 2010, p. 601). Thus, the central authority changed its military structure from land-holding military-based agents toward a stable army. The stable army caused an increasing burden on the state revenues. The central authority had to allocate a share for military organization. As Yavuz Cezar (2000) argued that the central authority reserved a small share for military expenditures from the central budget. The new situation increased the need for financial resources in cash instead of tax revenues in kind. The changes in military organizations, in this sense, were one of the most important outcomes of changing economic environments toward monetary-based economies from the sixteenth century.

Another small institutional difference emerged in contract durations. The administrative/military-based agents had the right to manage timar contracts if they served in the military organization of the empire. The tax-farming contracts, however, had limited contract duration from one year to 12 years (Darling, 1996, p. 135; Karaman & Pamuk, 2010, p. 601; Salzmann, 1993, p. 339). The limited duration contracts entailed the emergence of more complex contractual structures between the central authority and its agents. Complex structures caused higher transaction costs within the structure of law that caused divergence with European societies (Chapter 5). The limited duration contracts directed agents to maximize their revenues in the short term. The central authority was also compelled to increase its financial resources in short terms due to the exogenous shocks. Thus, shocks and the rules of the games enabled the central authority to terminate contracts by using its coercive power (Chapter 6). The changing structure of agents from administrative/military-based agents to non-state agents decreased risks in favor of the central authority when it chose to renege (*müsadere*) on contracts (Arslantaş, 2019). The new group of agents, however, preferred to behave opportunistically to recover their investments on tax-farming contracts. Limited contract durations and increasing confiscatory behavior of the central authority created such incentives for the agents within the institutional environment. More importantly, the structure of law played a crucial role in limiting opportunistic behaviors of contracting parties during the early modern period.

The failure of tax-farming institutions entailed higher budget deficits during the first half of the seventeenth century. The competition over economic privileges of contractual relations caused violence and uprisings supported by powerful groups during the first half of the seventeenth century. The violence mostly deteriorated production and tax collecting due to the increasing banditry. The unemployed agents within the timar institution were the main players of disturbance in Anatolia regions. The production was significantly disrupted as producers left their lands. In addition to slowing growth rates in territorial expansion, the central authority faced inadequate financial resources from the last decades of the sixteenth century. The budget deficits emerged during the same period. The seventeenth century was the period of increasing economic, political, and military competition with European societies. The emergence of tax-farming institutions was a part of this competition in addition to changing economic and political environments.

In the second half of the century, budget deficits decreased when the effects of the *Jalali Revolts* started to diminish in the Ottoman economy. The central authority imposed new rules over the tax-farming institution. The main purpose was to direct agents to invest in their contracts and to increase financial resources during the eighteenth century (Genç, 2000, p. 113). The first change emerged in the contract durations. As long as the agents lived, they had the right to manage financial resources under the lifetime tax-farming institution (Karaman & Pamuk, 2010, p. 603; Pamuk, 2004b, p. 17; Pamuk, 2009, p. 22). The central authority expected that longer durations created incentive mechanisms for productive activities. The emergence of the lifetime tax-farming institution corresponded to the last years of the seventeenth century.

The increasing durations, however, entailed the emergence of a new kind of payment for the central budget. The agents had to pay an advance payment (*muaccele*), which was 10 or 12 times higher than annual payments in tax-farming contracts (Genç, 2000, p. 108; Karaman & Pamuk, 2010, p. 602). The advanced payments changed the direction of budget deficits from the last decades of the seventeenth century. More importantly, the first outcomes of longer duration contracts had positive effects on the state revenues. The central authority achieved a balanced budget toward the middle of the century (Fig. 4.1). Even if the central authority enforced long-term contracts with advance payments from the

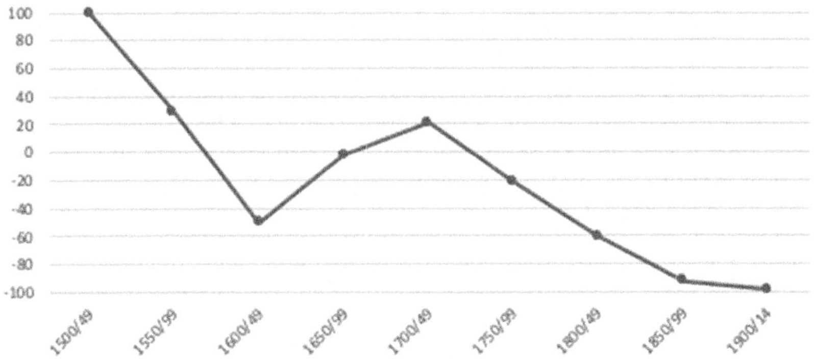


**Fig. 4.1** The trend of annual average budget deficits by sub-periods (in Silver, 1500/49 = 100) (*Source* This figure is generated from Genç and Özvar [2006])

beginning of the eighteenth century, budget deficits continued to increase until the nineteenth century. Although advance payments increased financial resources during the first decades of the century, the central authority continued to impose its confiscatory strategies with its coercive power. The increasing competition among provincial notables deepened the crisis over revenue extracting mechanisms and deteriorated the expected benefits of long-term contracts in the Ottoman Empire (Genç, 2000, p. 115). More importantly, the failures in revenue extracting institutions entailed divergence in terms of per capita GDP during the early modern period.

The process of institutional change brings a question out on why the Ottoman Empire faced inefficient economic outcomes and failed to establish efficient mechanisms from the seventeenth century. The theoretical background of institution change provides a crucial explanation of the economic failure of the Ottoman Empire during the early modern period. In a theoretical context, there are two main perspectives over institutional change. One argues that institutions do change in an evolutionary process. The evolution promotes efficient institutions and disables inefficient ones over time. The early modern period, however, imposes certain constraints over central authorities. The historical context shows that the Ottoman Empire had its limitations and boundaries that disabled the evolutionary process of institutional change.

The first constraint was related to the authority of Ottoman rulers within the institutional environment. The rulers had to maintain the traditional structure in the economic environment. The traditions, in this sense, limited the institutional change, particularly on property rights. State ownership was the dominant mechanism over property relations. The main reason was the obligation of the central authority to sustain the traditional structure of the empire. The central authority restricted private ownership for different reasons in addition to the traditional structure. The elimination of land-holding aristocracy entailed the emergence of two divergence groups. The first group consisted of agents, including administrative/military-based agents, judicial/religious-based agents, and provincial notables. The main characteristic of these groups was that they were exempt from tax. The second group included taxpayers. The Ottoman Empire gave importance to keep these social groups separate within the institutional structure. In other words, it was difficult for taxpayers to become members of the first group. This constraint prevented the central authority to impose private property on financial resources related to tax-farming institutions. The taxpayers had the usufruct rights over their lands within the state ownership. Once powerful groups started to privatize the financial resources, the taxpayers would face the risk of losing their lands. Furthermore, feudal relations started to emerge within the institutional environment. To preserve the allocation of resources, the central authority sustained state ownership in contractual relations. This kind of choice was related to collective action theories of institutional change. Higher-level rules determined the way of institutional change instead of the evolutionary process. Thus, the elimination of inefficient institutional structures was restricted, and hence, the inefficient institutional mechanisms dominated the institutional structures under contractual relations.

The second constraint was the increasing power of powerful groups from the beginning of the seventeenth century. The tax-farming institutions emerged within the same period with the *Jelali Revolts*. The violence that emerged in the first decades of the seventeenth century entailed changes in the balance of power among powerful groups. Judicial/religious-based agents and non-state agents (provincial notables) achieved to decrease the power of administrative-military-based agents within the institutional environment. The substantial proportion of tax-farming contracts belonged to the non-state agents with the increasing power of judicial/religious-based agents. The key was these groups prevented the central authority from imposing the efficient rules of the game within the institutional change process. The judicial/religious-based agents could gain revenues through courts in the allocation of contracts. Their collusion with provincial notables created mutual economic interests that entailed increasing opportunistic behaviors in contractual relations (Chapter 5). Thus, higher-level rules limited the effects of institutional change and restricted the emergence of efficient institutional mechanisms.

The failure of tax-farming institutions entailed an institutional change at the end of the seventeenth century. The limited duration contracts directed agents toward opportunistic behaviors. The institutional change process faced similar constraints. The rules of the game changed, but these changes caused increasing power of judicial/religious-based agents and non-state agents during the eighteenth century. The central authority allocated contracts with longer durations to create incentive mechanisms for promoting investments in financial resources. Each agent had the right to keep their contracts as long as they lived (Genç, 2000, p. 107). Yet, the lifetime tax-farming contracts prevented the institutional structure from emerging private ownership. The State ownership continued to dominate the institutional environment. Furthermore, the role of judicial/religious-based agents increased in allocating lifetime tax-farming contracts. The main obstacle to the emergence of private ownership and limited contract durations was the increasing power of judicial/religious-based agents during the eighteenth century. The *müsadere* (confiscation) allowed the central authority to change its agents without any explicit costs. The judicial/religious-based agents could gain revenues through their courts in allocating new lifetime tax-farming contracts. Once private ownership emerged in the Ottoman Empire, the courts faced losing influence on financial resources. Even if the central authority recognized the importance of institutional change, this process was deteriorated by other higher-level rules. Thus, the institutional change became restricted and limited in the early modern period.

The exogenous shocks and subsequent endogenous dynamics directed the Ottoman Empire to change its institutional structure from the first decades of the seventeenth century. As it was given above, institutions do change in two main different ways. The first was based on the collective actions of powerful groups. The second emerged as a spontaneous order. Each perspective provided theoretical background in examining the institutional change that emerged in the Ottoman Empire. The recent literature, however, had deficiencies in explaining the reason behind why the central authority chose to allocate contracts under tax-farming institutions. This literature mostly focused on increasing needs for financial resources due to the exogenous shocks. The other side of the coin showed different reasons based on endogenous dynamics. The balance of power through contractual relations was overlooked in examining the economic performance of the Ottoman Empire. More importantly, the role of law and judicial decisions were two of the most important non-economic institutions in the long-run economic development. The historical context presented that higher-level rules determined by the way of institutional change instead of the evolutionary process. Thus, inefficient institutions were promoted within the institutional environment for preserving the interests of certain groups. As it was argued in collective action theories, the elimination of inefficient institutions was difficult once powerful groups intervened in the institutional change process.

The tax-farming contracts were related not only to revenue-extracting but also to judicial decisions. Law enforcement was a crucial mechanism within the contractual relations. Actions taken by judicial/religious-based agents should be considered as an important variable in contractual relations. The recent literature argued that the powerful groups failed to limit the absolute and coercive power of the central authority. What did the literature miss that these powerful groups intended to restrict the opportunistic behaviors of the central authority? Was the opportunistic behavior of the central authority providing an advantage for powerful groups within the institutional change process? Was the institutional change process a relationship based on self-interest? The examination of judicial decisions over tax-farming contracts was crucial to answering such questions. This kind of analysis promised to fulfill the gap in the recent literature over the economic performance of the Ottoman Empire during the early modern period.

## References

Afyoncu, E. Zeamet. *İslam Ansiklopedisi*, 44, 162–164.

Arslantaş, Y. (2019). Making sense of müsadere practice, state confiscation of elite wealth, in the Ottoman Empire, circa 1453–1839. *History Compass, 17*(6), e12548.

Barkan, Ö. L. (1980). *Türkiye'de Toprak Meselesi / Toplu Eserler 1.* Gözlem Yayınları.

Barkey, K. (1994). *Bandits and bureaucrats: The Ottoman route to state centralization.* Cornell University Press.

Bolt, J., & Van Zanden, J. L. (2014). The Maddison project: Collaborative research on historical national accounts. *Economic History Review, 29*(2), 627–651.

Brandt, L., Ma, D., & Rawski, T. G. (2014). From divergence to convergence: Reevaluating the history behind china's economic boom. *Journal of Economic Literature, 52*(1), 45–123.

Broadberry, S., & Klein, A. (2012). Aggregate and per capita GDP in Europe, 1870–2000: Continental, regional and national data with changing boundaries. *Scandinavian Economic History Review, 60*(1), 79–107.

Bulut, M., & Altay, B. (2021). The Ottoman economy (1870–1913): Preliminary second-generation estimates. *Turkish Journal of Islamic Economies, 8*(2), 1–24. https://doi.org/10.26414/A485

Cezar, Y. (2000). *Osmanlı Maliyesi'nde Değişim ve Bunalım Dönemi*. Alan.

Çizakça, M. (1996). *A comparative evolution of business partnerships: The Islamic world and Europe, with specific reference to the Ottoman archives*. E. J. Brill.

Darling, L. (1996). *Revenue-raising and legitimacy: Tax collecting and finance administration in the Ottoman Empire, 1560–1660*. E. J. Brill.

Genç, M., & Özvar, E. (2006). *Osmanlı Maliyesi: Kurumlar ve Bütçeler, 2*. Osmanlı Bankası ve Araştırma Merkezi.

Genç, M. (2000). *Osmanlı İmparatorluğu'nda Devlet ve Ekonomi*. Ötüken Neşriyat.

Hoffman, P. T. (2015). *Why did Europe conquer the world?* Princeton University Press.

İnalcık, H. (2018). *The Ottoman Empire: Sultan, society and economy*. Kronik.

Karaman, K. (2009). Decentralized coercion and self-restraint in provincial taxation: The Ottoman Empire, 15th–16th centuries. *Journal of Economic Behavior & Organization, 71*(3), 690–703.

Karaman, K. K., & Pamuk, Ş. (2010). Ottoman state finances in European perspective. *The Journal of Economic History, 70*(3), 593–629.

Karaman, K. K., & Pamuk, Ş. (2013). Different paths to the modern state in Europe: The interaction between warfare, economic structure and political regime. *American Political Science Review, 107*, 603–626.

Kennedy, P. (1988). *The rise and fall of the great powers*. Unwin Hyman Limited.

Ma, D., & Rubin, J. (2019). The paradox of power: Principal-agent problems and fiscal capacity in absolutist regimes. *Journal of Comparative Economics, 47*(2), 277–294.

Maddison, A. (2001). *The world economy: A millennial perspective*. OECD Publishing.

Maddison, A. (2003). *The world economy: Historical statistics*. OECD Publishing.

Pamuk, Ş. (2000). *A monetary history of the Ottoman Empire*. Cambridge University Press.

Pamuk, Ş. (2004a). Institutional change and the longevity of the Ottoman Empire, 1500–1800. *The Journal of Interdisciplinary History, 35*(2), 225–247.

Pamuk, Ş. (2004b). The evolution of Ottoman financial institutions, 1600–1914. *Financial History Review, 11*(1), 7–32.

Pamuk, Ş. (2009). Changes in factor markets in the Ottoman Empire 1500–1800. *Continuity and Change, 24*(1), 1–30.

Pamuk, Ş. (2018). *Uneven Centuries: Economic Development of Turkey since 1820.* Princeton University Press.

Rubin, J. (2017). *Rulers, religion, and riches: Why the west got rich and the Middle East did not?* Cambridge University Press.

Salzmann, A. (2004). *Tocqueville in the Ottoman Empire: Rival paths to the modern state.* E. J. Brill.

Salzmann, A. (1993). An Ancien regime revisited: "Privatization" and political economy in the eighteenth-century Ottoman Empire. *Politics & Society, 21*(4), 393–423.

Tabakoğlu, A. (2008). *Türkiye İktisat Tarihi.* Dergah.

Tezcan, B. (2010). *The second Ottoman Empire: Political and social transformation in the early modern world.* Cambridge University Press.

Tilly, C. (1990). *Coercion, capital and European states, AD 990–1992.* Princeton University Press.

Van Zanden, J. L. (2009). *The long road to the industrial revolution, the European economy in a global perspective, 1000–1800.* E. J. Brill.

Yaycioglu, A. (2016). *Partners of the empire, the crisis of the Ottoman order in the age of revolutions.* Stanford University Press.

CHAPTER 5

# Legal-Economic Structure of Tax-Farming Contracts

**Abstract** This chapter gives the legal structure of tax-farming contracts, including prices, contract durations, conditions, and liabilities of contracting parties. Furthermore, this chapter presents the structure of agents and their changes from the beginning of the sixteenth century to the nineteenth century. The changing structure of agents reflects changing institutional structures and the level of the rule of law. This chapter has also incorporated the structure of law and the role of judicial/religious-based agents into the analysis. Recent literature has argued that judges were responsible for executing auctions and approving entitlements (*berats*) of the highest bidder agents. One of the main contributions of this study is based on the role of judges in contractual relations. Even if a few researchers have focused on the actions taken by judges within the institutional environment, these studies have overlooked the problem of why the perception of these groups of agents changed and how these groups achieved to determine the path of institutional change to protect their interests. This chapter has suggested that judges played a crucial role in the emergence of the rule of law for elites.

**Keywords** The Ottoman Empire · Limited access order · Judicial decision · Changing structure of agents · The rule of law for elites



B. Altay and F. Oğuz, *Rules, Contracts and Law Enforcement in the Ottoman Empire*, Palgrave Studies in Institutions, Economics and Law, https://doi.org/10.1007/978-3-030-79577-1_5

The tax-farming institutions dominated the economic environment in the Ottoman Empire as the main contract form in agriculture and trade. The central authority extracted substantial shares of its revenues through contracts beginning with the sixteenth century. The contractual relations were based on more complex relations in addition to revenue extracting. The Ottoman Empire was a typical representative sample of limited access order during the early modern period. The evolutionary process of tax-farming institutions was compatible with the changes in the state structure. Institutional change, in this sense, included not only changes in economic structures but also political and legal structures. The tax-farming contracts and the rules determined through coalitions provided explicit and systematic information on how the institutional structure changed over time and why the existing institutions emerged as they did in the Ottoman Empire.

This part focuses on tax-farming contracts as a source of examining the legal structure of the Ottoman Empire and analyzing the role of law over economic performance in the early modern period. To incorporate the law into the long-run economic analysis of the Ottoman Empire, this study includes more than 400 contracts covering, with lapses, the 300 years from the first decades of the sixteenth century to the last decades of the eighteenth century. The commitment problems that emerged in contractual relations generate the role of law and legal structures within the institutional environment. Law enforcement determines the choice sets and behaviors of contracting parties. Inefficient enforcement mechanisms direct individuals to behave opportunistically in their actions. Furthermore, monitoring mechanisms through legal institutions (Sharia Courts in the Ottoman Empire) restricts possible opportunism within the institutional environment. In this sense, this study also employs Ottoman Sharia Court records to show actions taken by contracting parties. Incorporating court records into analysis allows us to present the correlation between the rules of the games (written rules in contracts) and their enforcements under the institutional structure. The data presented below shows that a commitment problem emerged in contractual relations by differences in intended and actual durations. The court records provide information on how contracting parties defected within the games. It is difficult to argue that the only reason for commitment problems was based on the absolute and coercive power of the central authority. It will be argued that the powerful groups had limited ability to constraint power of the central authority by collusion.

The court registers are useful to determine the strategies and actions of contracting parties. This study employs court registers from different territories of the Ottoman Empire, covering the 300 years from 1500 to 1800. These registers mostly include why the tax-farming contracts passed in other hands. More importantly, court registers provide information on how contracting parties deviated from their commitments determined in tax-farming contracts. The data shows that the commitment problem emerged not only from exogenous shocks but also changing endogenous dynamics within the institutional environment.

The court registers present that the first deviation arises not only from the absolute power of the central authority but also from the opportunistic behavior of powerful contracting groups. To show possible deviations of contracting parties, this study employed the microfilm copies of Sharia Courts from different provinces stored in the National Library of Turkey. The Sharia Court records mostly begin in the 1500s and encompass the period between the sixteenth century to the end of the First World War. The court registers that covered the sixteenth century contain judicial decisions over disputes of tax-farming contracts only sporadically. Nevertheless, each court registers present possible strategies of contracting parties. Thus, we choose to classify dominant strategies of contracting parties by examining each court register. This classification is based on the density of strategies. To give more details about judicial decisions, this study presents examples by using microfilms including the most used court decisions.

Prepared by judges, court registers provide detailed information about the socio-economic structure of an individual at the time of actions taken, including the title of the contracting party, strategies, and actions. The title of the contracting party is crucial to examine judicial biases in legal decisions. The titles of the powerful individuals are also related to how tax-farming contracts were allocated by the central authority. In examining the socio-economic structure of contracting parties, this study also utilizes secondary sources that focused on contractual relations during the same period. Incorporating secondary sources also enriches the changing structure of partnerships and collusion among contracting parties. The cooperation among different groups is crucial to examine the changing balance of power between powerful groups and the central authority.

Both primary and secondary sources argue that these partnerships and collusion included not only written and explicit contracts but also implicit relations. The judicial decisions, in some cases, are based on these implicit contractual relations among powerful groups. Thus, both tax-farming contracts and judicial decisions provide historical evidence to examine why the Ottoman Empire failed to establish rule of law during the early modern period. An analysis of economic institutions should be expanded with non-economic institutions (legal institutions) to show the divergence between Western Europe and the Middle East. This is because societies may employ similar economic institutions such as contracts, but the small institutional differences that emerged from non-economic institutions determined the long-run economic performances.

The central authority chose to allocate state offices under contractual relations. The dominant mechanism was to establish partnerships with powerful groups during the early modern period. These partnerships through contractual relations were an important doorstep condition toward establishing the rule of law. Despite the significant body of literature that has focused on the contractual relations between the central authority and powerful groups, studies on the legal structure and its theoretical background have been slow to progress. The question of why the Ottoman Empire failed to establish the rule of law even though similar mechanisms were employed in Western European societies has been put aside by the recent literature. The main culprit is that the recent literature accepted the structure of law as given. The contractual relations, however, should be considered as a part of dynamic change in the perception of agents.

The institutional change emerged due to the exogenous shocks but changing rules of the game was part of continuing interactions among contracting parties. As long as the central authority was one of the dominant parties in tax-farming contracts, its choices directed the other party to develop different mechanisms in preventing their economic privileges from opportunistic behavior of the coercive power. In this sense, what the recent literature overlooked in examining contractual relations was that each research accepted the absolute power and opportunism of the state as given. As it was given in historical context, tax-farming contracts surrounded substantial shares of the state revenues. The contractual relations through interactions among parties determined the way of economic performances.

This part focuses on two different perspectives. First, the law and enforcement mechanisms are not accepted as given. Secondly, the absolute power of the central authority is not accepted as given. Each variable is part of negotiations and bargaining among contracting parties. It is assumed that if the central authority was willing to use its coercive power, it would emerge due to the actions taken by other parties. In this sense, the strategies of powerful groups are considered as outcomes of the choices of the central authority. The court records and judicial decisions provide information to analyze the strategies of contracting parties and deviations from the rules of the game. Tax-farming contracts present quantitative variables, including changing prices and contract durations. The court records, however, contain action taken by the contracting parties. More importantly, court records allow examining strategies during periods of exogenous shocks.

As was mentioned above, this study chose to employ the NWW perspective in explaining the role of law and legal structures on the economic performance of the Ottoman Empire. Before getting a deeper analysis of tax-farming contracts and judicial decisions, it would be useful to generate a connection between the theoretical and historical backgrounds. The Ottoman Empire was a typical form of "limited access order" from a theoretical perspective. The historical context contained certain features that the Ottoman Empire commonly used its courts to sustain order. From a theoretical perspective, the order of the NWW perspective was to sustain order and decrease violence in society. The main purpose of the rulers was to allocate economic and political privileges toward powerful groups. If the self-interest of powerful groups was intact within the institutional environment, violence stayed at low levels. The allocation of privileges was a common strategy. On the way to the rule of law, this was one of the most important dominant strategies of the rulers. Despite the significant body of early modern states choosing to establish partnerships with powerful groups, the legal structure was the crucial determinant of small institutional differences. The legal protection for powerful groups should be imposed and credibly enforced by the central authority.

First, the "rule of law for elites", in this sense, became an important doorstep condition. The legal protection for elites enabled these groups to honor their commitments, and more importantly, provided strong political support for the central authority. The rents allocated through contracts entailed limited access to financial resources—labor, capital, land—in favor of powerful groups. If their rents would be protected by the law, powerful groups had a strong incentive to sustain partnerships with the central authority. Different powerful groups dominated the tax-farming contract market, including the *timar* institution, from the first decades of the Ottoman Empire. The domination of powerful groups was related to the economic conditions of socio-economic groups.

The rapid territorial expansion provided substantial financial resources for the members of military organizations. Furthermore, the military campaigns allowed Ottoman rulers to allocate certain titles in addition to *timar* contracts. Establishing partnerships with military members was the dominant strategy because of their control over soldiers and roles in territorial expansion. These were economic conditions of why the central authority mostly employed administrative/military-based agents under the *timar* institution. The legal structure, however, determined whether the Ottoman Empire achieved to establish the first doorstep condition or not. The rule of law for the elite condition should be determined through the legal structure.

Developing a central legal structure made the Ottoman Empire "limited access order". Sharia courts were parts of a highly centralized state structure. *Kadis* (judges) were the high authority of these courts, they formed the representative body of the state authority through courts. The Ottoman rulers directly assigned these judges to the Sharia courts. Sharia courts played a crucial role in the allocation of contracts. Under the *timar* institution, the Ottoman rulers gave the economic rights with an approval (*berat*), and those should be approved by Sharia courts. *Kadis* recorded each *berat* to the court records. Once a dispute emerged in *timar* contracts, Sharia courts had the power to enforce the law.

Disputes could emerge from two different circumstances. First, unemployed agents could put in a claim for a *timar* contract. Sharia courts had the authority to protect the interest of employed agents, and lower possible violence through formal rules. Secondly, taxpayers (*reaya*) had the chance to bring their complaints about agents to these courts. In other words, Sharia courts enabled taxpayers to submit a petition about their complaints. *Kadis* enforced the law regarding *berat* that included information about agents. The upshot was that Sharia courts provided information over the actions taken by agents within the contractual arrangements.

As it was given above, Sharia courts had an efficient role in territorial and economic expansion until the last decades of the sixteenth century. The central authority developed a multilateral monitoring mechanism under the *timar* institution. The monitoring mechanism was based on legal rights that were given to different groups in society. The first monitoring mechanism included the direct monitoring of agents during campaigns. Each agent employed through *timar* contracts had an obligation for participating in campaigns. These agents had to bring their registers consisting of economic activities under *timar* contracts. Thus, the central authority had the chance to directly monitor the activities of agents.

Secondly, the central authority employed state officials to tax collecting from different provinces. These state officials had the right to collect different taxes such as cizye, avarız, and port dues. Each official also investigated actions taken by agents within the contractual relations. These officials interviewed individuals they had chosen at random among taxpayers. If they found out serious complaints about agents, they had the right to bring them to trial through Sharia courts.

Finally, *Kadis* had the legal authority to directly monitor the actions of agents. Even if there were no complaints from the taxpayers, the judges could carry out their controls and record them in their courts. The three monitoring mechanisms within the legal structure directed administrative/military-based agents to cooperate with the central authority. The territorial expansion and efficient revenue extracting were the main outcomes of the centralized legal structure during the sixteenth century. The effectiveness of Sharia courts can also be determined in the counts of *timar* contracts during this period (See, for example, Barkan, 1980; İnalcik, 1994).

It was difficult to argue that there was a rule of law for elites under the timar institution. The timar contracts were based on cooperation among contracting parties. Both the central authority and its representatives needed each other during periods of rapid territorial expansion. The interests of contracting parties were economic. These economic interests, however, bounded to credible commitments. The central authority allocated *timar* contracts regarding a merit system. This merit system was a kind of monitoring and controlling mechanism within the legal structure. The administrative/military-based agents were able to obtain contracts if they were beneficial in campaigns.

Once the central authority chose to give a timar contract by ignoring the merit system, the violence could emerge from collective actions of administrative/military-based agents. The central authority, however, chose to allocate certain timar contracts toward different groups of agents, including judicial/religious-based agents and non-Muslim groups. The main reason was to sustain political order in strategic territories. Within

Balkan territories, the Ottoman rulers chose to establish such partnerships where non-Muslim populations were high during the sixteenth century. More importantly, they could impose a *Boycott* by refraining from participating in campaigns. The sixteenth century was the period that witnessed violence organized by military groups, including janissaries or timar holders, in collective action (Faroqhi, 1994). The strong cooperation among the members of administrative/military-based agents could limit the power of the central authority within the legal structure. The merit system was the building block for allocating contracts.

The Sharia courts were the representative body of the central authority that had the power to approve the legality of the rights (*berats*) that emerged from *timar* contracts. *Berat* was given by the central authority. However, the lawful use of these *Berats* was entirely under the supervision of the Sharia Courts and Judges. The central authority had the legal right to terminate *timar* contracts. This right was based on judicial decisions. The multilateral monitoring mechanism allowed judges to monitor the actions of administrative/military-based agents. Secondly, the law enabled taxpayers to bring their complaints about the illegitimate activities of agents. Judges had the authority to give a verdict over actions taken by the agents. The law determined the punishment for opportunistic behaviors.

The most common strategy of the central authority was to dismiss cheating agents from military organizations and confiscate their wealth. The central authority, however, imposed these strategies once the judicial decision was given and approved by the Sharia courts. The court approval on opportunistic behavior of a certain administrative/military-based agent directed the other agents to exclude the cheating agent. The possible violence and other collective actions such as *Boycotting the Ruler* stayed at low levels within the institutional environment. The Sharia Courts and the law, in this sense, played a crucial role in decreasing transaction costs. The written rules and judicial decisions provided information for other interest groups, and the legitimacy of judicial decisions from trials became an important building block of both territorial expansion and low violence in the Ottoman Empire. Thus, the institutional structure could not establish the "rule of law for elites" under the timar institution.

The second doorstep condition to the rule of law was perpetually lived forms of organizations established by powerful groups. The State was one of the most important organizations while perpetually lived private and public organizations established by powerful groups were other important organizations. As it was given above, the state structure of the

Ottoman Empire was highly integrated particularly from the conquest of Istanbul. What Mehmed II did was to strengthen the centralized political structure within the institutional environment. The abandonment of land-holding aristocracy in favor of powerful groups bestowed with titles entailed an integrated state structure compared to European states, including feudal states, city-states, and small principalities. Only France and England reflected political and economic structures and features of integrated states in Europe. More importantly, Sharia Courts and the law were crucial building blocks of the integrated state structure of the Ottoman Empire. The powerful groups of Mehmed II mostly consisted of administrative-military-based agents with titles. These groups increased their political influences until the last decades of the sixteenth century. As long as the main financial resources of the central authority were based on spoils of war and tax revenues of newly conquered territories, these groups increased their powers in state affairs (Çizakça, 1996; Darling, 1996). The most important feature of these military-based groups was their strong cooperation among each other, particularly under the *timar* institution. Each high-ranking bureaucrat was a part of the military organization. The members of military organizations imposed their political controls through *timar* contracts.

The cooperation among administrative/military-based agents, however, was based on implicit contracts and rules. These groups failed to establish perpetually lived public and private organizations to sustain their power in state affairs. Even if they achieved to establish certain private organizations called the cash waqfs, those had limited mechanisms to support the political power of administrative/military-based agents and their financial resources. The timar institution, in this sense, had deficiencies in the way of rule of law in the Ottoman Empire.

The institutional structure partially achieved second and third doorstep conditions. In the legal structure, the appointment of judges by the central authority remained an obstacle to doorstep conditions. Once the strong cooperation among administrative/military-based agents was disconcerted, the actions taken by judges became crucial in contractual relations. Changing the bargaining powers of powerful groups with the central authority entailed the emergence of different groups in contractual relations. With the effects of increasing transaction costs, the role of judges and courts could reverse the fortune of the Ottoman Empire. Therefore, things had changed, and more complex contractual relations, bargaining and negotiations, partnerships, and collusion emerged within the institutional environment.

The most crucial factor was the changing structure of agents and their perceptions from the seventeenth century. Nevertheless, as given below, the Ottoman Empire achieved to establish doorstep conditions toward the rule of law. But partial achievements emerged from small institutional differences in the legal structure that caused relative economic backwardness during the early-modern period.

What deteriorated cooperation among the central authority and its agents was a market failure in the contract market. As it was given above, exogenous shocks forced the central authority to develop different institutional mechanisms in allocating *timar* contracts in the first place. The dominant strategy was to give timar contracts from different territories. These contracts located far from Western Anatolia, Rumelia, and Balkan territories, included lower financial resources compared to contracts newly conquered territories in Western soils. Furthermore, the administrative/military-based agents who held contracts from Eastern territories faced economic problems due to the long-distance campaigns.

The changing military technology forced the Ottoman Empire to change its military organizations (Karaman & Pamuk, 2010). Cavalry troops lost their comparative advantage against rifle infantries of European states. The loss of military superiority in a way determined the natural borders of the Ottoman Empire during the seventeenth century. Slowing territorial expansion, in this sense, caused decreases in the supply of *timar* contracts. Being a member of the military organization was one of the most beneficial choices for subjects. The *timar* contracts provided financial resources for administrative/military-based agents in the previous century. The cash waqf established by these agents and probate records in Sharia courts showed that the wealthier groups of the Ottoman Empire mostly included individuals from administrative and military organizations. The growth rate of administrative/military-based agents exceeded the growth rate of territorial expansion as well as contracts supplied by the central authority.

The allocation of timar contracts deteriorated due to the changing military technology, changing economic environment entailed monetary problems within the Ottoman economy. The *timar* contracts mostly enabled tax revenues in kind instead of cash. The new trade routes toward the Far East and the flow of precious metals from the New World entailed changes in economic exchanges. Furthermore, the price levels increased from the last decades of the sixteenth century. The administrative/military-based agents faced increasing costs because of both long-duration campaigns and prices. The revenues of these agents, however, remained at the same levels for different reasons. First, spoils of war decreased with diminishing territorial expansion. Secondly, and more importantly, the central authority chose not to change shares of agents in contractual relations. Devaluations in Ottoman currencies and increasing prices entailed decreases in real wages (revenues) of the agents. Hence, the exogenous shocks changed endogenous dynamics as the structure of agents, perception of agents, and the rules of the game. The distinction in the legal structure has become more evident: *Sharia Law* and *Urfi Law*.

The exogenous shocks and changing endogenous dynamics forced the central authority to bend the law and the rules to sustain order within the economic and political environment. Institutions changed, the rules of the games evolved, the law and its enforcement shifted toward new forms regarding changes in state power. Sharia courts and their judges, however, had managed to maintain their position and even increase their influence in contractual relations.

The institutional change toward tax-farming contracts emerged from opportunistic behaviors of administrative/military-based agents of the former institution. The shortage in timar contracts caused corruption in allocating timar contracts. The merit system deteriorated by unemployed agents, who were willing to direct their financial resources to obtain timar contracts. The unemployed agents established partnerships (collusion) with high-ranking bureaucrats, located in Istanbul. Furthermore, judicial/religious-based agents started taking part in contractual relations within the timar institution. Once collusion was established between an agent and a high-ranking bureaucrat, the agent needed to take judicial approval (*Berat*) from Sharia courts.

Sharia courts were local courts established at the center of provinces. The central authority assigned the highest authority of courts from the center. In other words, the legitimacy of judges depended on the high-ranking bureaucrats of the central authority. This dependence entailed increasing personal relations among the authorities of the center and the periphery. In this sense, judicial/religious-based agents could be beneficial to be part of collusion rather than fight against administrative/military-based agents and their political supporters. The law remained stable, but collisions entailed changes in the direction of financial resources. The administrative/military-based agents were willing to transfer their financial resources to maintain their contracts or to obtain contracts from the central authority.

The central authority changed rules to solve two main problems that emerged within the institutional environment. First, increasing numbers of unemployed agents might cause violence in society. Second, the central authority faced losses in state revenues. Increasing costs due to the exogenous factors created the incentive for the administrative/military-based agents to crop higher shares from tax revenues. More importantly, financial resources devoted to establishing collusion within *timar* contracts caused destructive or unproductive outcomes in both the economy and military. Slowing territorial expansion ceased substantial revenues of the State. Collusion consumed and absorbed financial resources hindered investments of administrative/military-based agents on their contracts. As long as collusion increased within the institutional environment, the production and providing provisions for the army decreased within the economy.

The main purpose of the central authority was to develop rules and mechanisms that would eliminate such problems. The legal structure and the law remained stable in terms of revenue extracting contracts. The tax-farming contracts, in this sense, emerged from actions taken by administrative/military-based agents in contractual relations. The law-maintained property rights under absolute state ownership (Pamuk, 2009, p. 3). The central authority forced the administrative/military-based agents to direct their financial resources toward the central budget. To achieve this goal, the central authority imposed different mechanisms by changing the rules that organized contractual relations. The new rules and mechanisms entailed the emergence of more complex contracts and contractual relations.

To sum up, the transition from the timar institution toward tax-farming institution is based on exogenous shocks as well as endogenous dynamics. Deterioration in comparative advantages of administrative/military-based agents against European military power forced the central authority to change its military structure. While the territorial expansion started to slow down, the central authority faced difficulties in allocating contracts toward military-based agents. The demand for contracts exceeded the supply, and the shortage problem emerged in contract market within the institutional environment. More importantly, unemployed agents became a threat due to the increasing possibility of violence. The need of establishing a stable army changed coalition and partnership choices of the central authority. Increasing needs for cash capital for the costs of a stable army, the central authority developed a new mechanism to expand its financial resources (Pamuk, 2009). Thus, tax-farming contracts emerged as a domestic borrowing mechanism in the Ottoman Empire (Karaman & Pamuk, 2010). However, military-based agents had suffered from transferring financial resources to obtain these tax-farming contracts. Judicial/religious-based agents, in particular, started to organize the allocation of tax-farming contracts by establishing coalitions with local powerful groups and private financiers. Even if a substantial share of timar holders abandoned their contracts in exchange for obtaining tax-farming contracts, they failed to sustain their existence in the contract market. The rules of the game forced agents to find guarantors and higher financial resources. Thus, the structure of agents changed over time. With the emergence of new groups in contractual relations, the perception of agents also changed within the institutional environment.

The auction mechanism was the first and the most important change in the allocation of contracts. The merit system was abandoned in favor of the auction mechanism. By doing this way, the central authority developed a mechanism to direct the financial resources of the agents toward the central budget rather than establishing collusion. The courts in Istanbul had the authority to organize auctions and allocations of tax-farming contracts. Whoever offered the highest price for a contract, the court transferred economic privileges toward the highest bidder with judicial approval (*Berat*). The judges had a crucial role to maintain the role of courts in contract allocation under the tax-farming institution. The main reason was that courts gained substantial shares of revenues from contract approvals. More importantly, judges could increase their revenues through judicial approvals.

The allocation of tax-farming contracts spread toward Sharia courts in provinces. The growth of the tax-farming contract market caused the emergence of complex contractual relations. The higher complex relations, however, deteriorated the multilateral monitoring mechanism due to the changing structure of agents as well as changing perceptions. The complex contractual relations also emerged from changing economic conditions within the tax-farming contracts. Under the merit system, the administrative/military-based agents are committed to providing public goods within the *timar* contracts. Their financial capacities were not important in the distribution of contracts and fulfillment of commitments.

What changed the perception of agents was the changing economic conditions in tax-farming contracts.

The primary reason behind imposing the auction mechanism was to direct the financial resources of agents toward the central budget. Collusions emerged under the *timar* institution started to absorb financial resources of administrative/military-based agents in obtaining contracts. The central authority reversed the way these financial resources devoted opportunistic behaviors toward its benefits. The auction mechanism, however, allowed different groups to participate in contractual relations.

During the first decades of the tax-farming institution, administrative/military-based agents continued to dominate the contract market. This group of agents became the wealthiest group, particularly under the domination of the *timar* institution. The probate records located in Sharia courts and the cash waqfs established by individuals provided a series of information over the wealth of different socio-economic groups. The sixteenth-century Ottoman Empire encouraged being members of military organizations with its institutional structure and mechanisms. The administrative/military-based agents could achieve capital accumulation through military campaigns and *timar* contracts. Other important groups, including judicial/religious-based agents, producers, and merchants, had limited capacity for accumulating capital due to the rules of the game. Judicial/religious-based agents had the right to charge for their judicial services. Even if some of them achieved to obtain *timar* contracts, their revenues were dependent on judicial services.

This period also provided limited financial resources for producers and merchants. The central authority restricted foreign trade for two main reasons. First, *provisionalism* was one of the most important policies of the central authority (Genç, 2000). The main purpose was to provide provisions and goods for society. The provision of Istanbul and other cities was the priority in the allocation of provisions and goods. If there was a surplus after the allocation of produced goods, the central authority allowed merchants and producers for foreign trade. Secondly, the central authority banned producers and merchants from a foreign trade of strategic goods (Bulut, 2009). The main aim of the central authority was not to restrict the commercial activities of producers and merchants. The primary goal was to limit the resources of potential rival states, located in Europe and the Middle East, which had limited capacity to produce provisions for military campaigns.

The institutional change, however, changed the structure of agents. Once territorial expansion began to slow down, administrative/military-based agents suffered from limited financial resources. The spoils of war decreased. More importantly, increasing numbers of agents forced the central authority to allocate small-scale contracts. The decreasing revenues and the auction mechanism became costly transactions for the administrative/military-based agents. Wealthier members of this group of agents abandoned their *timar* contracts in favor of tax-farming contracts. The others, with higher financial resources, directed their financial resources to obtain tax-farming contracts through auctions. However, lower-level agents, with insufficient financial resources, faced difficulties to adapt themselves to the new institutional environment.

The monetary-based economy created an incentive mechanism for the central authority to promote tax-farming institutions (Tabakoğlu, 2008; Tezcan, 2010). The abandonment of the timar institution in favor of the tax-farming institution, therefore, changed the rules of the game (Pamuk, 2004). The new rules based on increasing monetary-based relations entailed the emergence of new groups of agents within the contract market. The new institutional structure, in this sense, emerged for adopting Ottoman economic structure into the new economic and political environment. Monetary-based economic exchanges played a crucial role because of the increasing need for financial resources in cash. More importantly, the new institutional structure emerged to decrease the transaction costs of the new economic and political environment of the Ottoman Empire.

The emergence of natural boundaries or small-scale changes in boundaries entailed a higher stationary economic structure. The revenues from spoils of war decreased, and the land-based military order disintegrated. The comparative advantage of land-based military order diminished against European foes. Increasing needs for a stable army caused the emergence of new financial items within the Ottoman budget. A stable army should be established, but their payments were based on wages or salaries instead of shares from tax revenues. The upshot was that the central authority imposed new rules to change its institutional structure. Higher-level rules were the main source of the tax-farming institution.

Did institutional change achieve to solve increasing transaction costs of the new economic and political environment? If one chose to examine this question through budget deficits, the main answer was that the Ottoman Empire achieved to increase its revenues or to decrease costs during the seventeenth century. Until the nineteenth century, however, the explicit data showed that the budget deficits exceeded the level of the first decades of the sixteenth century. In other words, the budget deficits became heavier compared to periods of violence and revolts in the Ottoman Empire.

The structure of law and its agents caused partial institutional change during the seventeenth and eighteenth centuries. The judicial/religious-based agents increased their political power from the seventeenth century. Revolts and violence entailed shifts in the balance of power. With the decreasing power of military-based agents due to the revolts and violence they caused, judicial/religious-based agents increased their influence on economic and political structures through Sharia courts. The main strategy of these groups of agents was to maintain the traditional structure of the law. In this sense, judicial/religious-based agents exerted considerable pressure to keep property rights under state ownership. This pressure was effective on the central authority, which chose to employ these groups of agents to propagate its rules over the society. In other words, the central authority constructed its legitimacy through Sharia courts and judicial/religious-based agents. The Sharia courts continued to be the approval authority of tax-farming contracts. The economic interests were to be protected for both courts and judicial/religious-based agents.

The changes in the balance of power in favor of judicial/religious-based agents increased judicial bias in Ottoman courts. As long as judicial/religious-based agents were one of the main parts of the multilateral monitoring mechanisms, they had the power to manipulate the monitoring capacity of the central authority. And they did. They first established collusion with high-ranking bureaucrats (mostly administrative/military-based agents with honorific titles) to increase their political efficiency within the territories. Those high-ranking bureaucrats and administrative-based agents were willing to obtain tax-farming contracts. What they were not willing to do was to leave Istanbul. Thus, the contracting agents employed secondary agents from powerful groups of provinces.

The provincial notables became important partners of tax-farming contracts in time (Pamuk, 2004, p. 229; Pamuk, 2009, p. 2; Yaycioglu, 2016). These groups had better information about the economic and geographic conditions of provinces. More importantly, they had better information about people who lived in provinces. The secondary agents, called provincial notables, also increased their political power through partnerships with primary agents. Judicial/religious-based agents, however, played a crucial role in such contractual arrangements between the primary and secondary agents. As long as judicial/religious-based agents vouched, local elites could be involved in contractual relationships. Provincial notables had to offer the highest price to primary agents to capture economic privileges of tax-farming contracts. The judicial/religious-based agents organized these auctions, and they made sure about the wealth of provincial notables through courts. The judicial/religious-based agents, in this sense, became an important monitoring mechanism of primary agents in exchange for protecting their economic interests within the institutional environment.

The implicit relationship between the primary agents (high-ranking bureaucrats) and judicial/religious-based agents was the building block for the "rule of law for elites" in the Ottoman Empire. The exogenous shocks forced the central authority to ignore such collusion up to a point. As long as they assured to transfer a certain amount of tax revenues toward the central budget, the central authority was willing to protect the interests of such powerful groups. The revolts and violence in the early seventeenth century should have triggered such a decision. The only exception emerged when an external shock hit the economy. In this situation, a conflict of interest forced the contracting parties to impose different strategies in contractual relations. The structure of law, however, maintained the balance of power in favor of judicial/religious-based agents under such circumstances. Their role in propagating rules and sustaining the legitimacy of the central authority through preserving traditions limited institutional change during the eighteenth century.

The recent literature argued that the eighteenth century was the period of major economic, political, and institutional transformations in the Ottoman Empire. This argument had its right when the economic transition from tax-farming institution to the lifetime tax-farming institution was considered. The structure of law, however, faced few changes during this period. The frozen structure of the law based on traditions and Sharia was maintained by judicial/religious-based agents in the eighteenth century. The rules of the game changed but this change was partial. The partiality was for protecting the interests of judicial groups. Judicial bias continued at increasing paces (Coşgel & Ergene, 2013; Kuran & Rubin, 2018).

The powerful groups became more powerful, and more importantly, provincial notables had the chance to eliminate the role of high-ranking bureaucrats, including mostly administrative/military-based agents in Istanbul, within the institutional environment. Some provincial notables increased their power at a level in which they could establish direct communication with Ottoman rulers. Secondary agents (provincial notables) achieved to increase their financial resources through contracts. The secondary agents obtained higher power relative to other secondary agents that gained their power through establishing comparative advantage in relations with judicial/religious-based agents. Courts and judicial/religious-based agents achieved to establish different mechanisms in their relations with the central authority. They chose not to use their comparative advantage on violence.

The new institutional structures and contractual relations changed the perception of judicial/religious-based agents. These groups of agents had an established knowledge of the dependence of central authority toward traditions and Sharia. Once decentralization increased its effects in controlling large territories, the central authority preferred to abide by the traditions and religious orientations. A very small number of judicial/religious-based agents became direct partners of tax-farming contracts and lifetime tax-farming contracts. But most of them chose to organize contractual relations through Sharia courts and their religious power. This kind of power restricted not only the central authority but also provincial notables within the institutional environment. No matter how close a provincial notable or high-ranking bureaucrat was to the central government, judges' detecting opportunistic behavior through the courts could have caused these groups to lose their contracts and even all their wealth.

The following chapter gives more detailed information on the contractual relations between the central authority and its agents. This chapter also focuses on contracts from both primary and secondary sources. The contracts provide information on the conditions of tax-farming and lifetime tax-farming contracts. These conditions also allow us to establish a systematic approach to examine the liabilities of contracting parties. In short, contracts determine the rules of the game. The changing conditions and liabilities also show that the structure of law should not be taken as given by the Ottoman Empire. The contracts present that the law depended on actions taken by contracting parties and decisions made in the short run. The institutional structure and the rules are dynamic regarding the contracts and actions taken by the contracting parties. The dynamic changes and strategies of contracting parties, however, will be presented with a systematic and analytical perspective under a game-theoretical model in Chapter 7.

## References


Barkan, Ö. L. (1980). *Türkiye'de Toprak Meselesi / Toplu Eserler 1.* Gözlem Yayınları.

Bulut, M. (2009). Reconsidering a classical Empire and a nation-state. *American Journal of Economics and Sociology, 68*(3), 791–828.

Çizakça, M. (1996). *A comparative evolution of business partnerships: The Islamic world and Europe, with specific reference to the Ottoman archives.* Leiden: Brill.

Coşgel, M., & Ergene, B. (2013). The selection bias in court records: Settlement and trial in eighteenth-century Ottoman Kastamonu. *The Economic History Review, 67*(2), 517–534.

Darling, L. (1996). *Revenue-raising and legitimacy: Tax collection and finance administration in the Ottoman Empire 1560–1660.* Leiden: Brill.

Faroqhi, S. (1994). Crisis and change, 1590–1699. In H. İnalcık (Ed.), *An economic and social history of the Ottoman Empire* (pp. 411–636).

Genç, M. (2000). *Osmanlı İmparatorluğu'nda Devlet ve Ekonomi.* Ötüken Neşriyat.

İnalcik, H. (1994). *An economic and social history of the Ottoman Empire, 1300–1914.* Cambridge University Press.

Karaman, K. K., & Pamuk, Ş. (2010). Ottoman state finances in European perspective. *The Journal of Economic History, 70*(3), 593–629.

Kuran, T., & Rubin, J. (2018). The financial power of the powerless: Interest rates and socioeconomic status under partial rule of law. *Economic Journal, 128*(609), 758–796.

Pamuk, Ş. (2004). Institutional change and the longevity of the Ottoman Empire, 1500–1800. *The Journal of Interdisciplinary History, 35*(2), 225–247.

Pamuk, Ş. (2009). Changes in factor markets in the Ottoman Empire 1500–1800. *Continuity and Change, 24*(1), 1–30.

Tabakoğlu, A. (2008). *Türkiye İktisat Tarihi.* Dergah.

Tezcan, B. (2010). *The second Ottoman Empire: Political and social transformation in the early modern world.* Cambridge University Press.

Yaycioglu, A. (2016). *Partners of the empire, the crisis of the Ottoman order in the age of revolutions.* Stanford University Press.

CHAPTER 6

# Analysis of Tax-Farming Contracts

**Abstract** This chapter presents a descriptive analysis of the tax-farming contracts, including prices, annual payments, actual and intended durations, between 1500 and 1800. The prices and annual payments given in contracts are in Ottoman currencies, and they reflect nominal values. To obtain more accurate data, each variable will be converted into real values in terms of silver with the prices of 1913. This chapter, however, has focused on two different variables from tax-farming contracts. The differences between intended and actual durations have formed first explicit data in examining the failure of the contractual relations. The findings have shown that a substantial proportion of tax-farming contracts had been terminated before the intended duration due to the exogenous shocks and endogenous dynamics. The theoretical background has suggested that deteriorated monitoring mechanisms and partial institutional change entailed commitment problems in contractual relations. Changing rules have been inadequate to solve commitment problems. The motivation of the central authority in maximizing revenues through auction mechanisms has directed agents to transfer their financial resources toward tax-farming contracts. The findings have also suggested that agents were mostly willing to take tax-farming contracts for political privileges. In sum, collusion among high-ranking bureaucrats of the central authority and agents has entailed contracts to change hands frequently. The second explicit data employed within this chapter have



B. Altay and F. Oğuz, *Rules, Contracts and Law Enforcement in the Ottoman Empire*, Palgrave Studies in Institutions, Economics and Law, https://doi.org/10.1007/978-3-030-79577-1_6

supported the assumptions over the differences between intended and actual durations. Our sample has presented that only 1/3 of tax-farming contracts had increasing prices during the auctions. The prices of other contracts have remained at the same level or decreased during the auctions. The recent literature has overlooked these two economic data that emerged from tax-farming contracts. The literature has considered this problem as a loss of state revenues in the long run. This study, however, has suggested that the rule of law for elites emerged within the institutional environment, and the judges played a crucial role in establishing this through judicial bias. Furthermore, it has been argued that the judges had enough motivation to promote the rule of law for elites.

**Keywords** The Ottoman Empire · Tax-farming contracts · Contract durations · Contract prices · Judges

Tax-farming contracts spread over the entire vast territory of the Ottoman Empire, from Yemen to Dubrovnik during the early modern period. The central authority found it beneficial to both maintain political authority and carry out economic activities through delegates. Despite the lapses in primary sources of tax-farming contracts, the sample of this study covered contracts from the different regions of the empire. Employing tax-farming contracts, however, had both its advantages and disadvantages in favor of the central authority. The rules determined in contracts seemed to be efficient in terms of economic purposes. The primary culprit was the lack of commitment problem between the contracting parties. Despite the significant body of growing literature that accumulated on the role of tax-farming institutions over state finance, research on the reasons behind the failure of contract relations had been slow to progress. There had been significant research on how contracts were established between the central authority and its agents, and which conditions surrounded the tax-farming contracts within the institutional structure. The absence of theoretical approaches to these contracts prevented researchers from studying the long-term evolution of economic structure. Why did the tax-farming contracts fail during the early modern period?

The analysis of this simple question is related to the concept of the rule of law. Two economic variables provide information in examining the relationship between the structure of law and economic performance. Contracts are an important part of the legal structure. Contractual arrangements, however, are insufficient to establish efficient outcomes in contractual relations. Law enforcement, therefore, has a crucial role in the emergence of efficient outcomes. Cooperative solutions generate one of the most important building blocks of efficiency. Thus, the law should force contracting parties to honor their commitments within the institutional environment.

The tax-farming contracts, in this sense, shed some light on the role of legal structure and actions taken by contracting parties within the contractual relations. The first indicator is contract durations. The tax-farming contracts show that there were two different contract durations: intended duration and actual durations. Intended durations are determined at the beginning of the contractual arrangement. Primary sources on tax-farming contracts show that intended durations were between 1 and 9 years during the sixteenth and seventeenth centuries. These primary sources also indicate there was an increasing pattern in the intended duration of contracts. This probably results from diverse endogenous factors. The short-term contracts, 1-year contracts may create incentives for rent-seeking behaviors. From a theoretical perspective, these contracts direct contracting parties to establish collusions.

Once an agent invests in a tax-farming contract, this agent gains not only economic but also political privileges. The honorific titles in Ottoman society provide substantial financial resources and considerable wealth. Such incentives force the agents to develop different mechanisms for protecting their interests from exogenous shocks and rival groups. The intended duration of tax-farming contracts shows that the central authority recognized the problems that emerged in contractual relations due to the short-term contracts. Figure 6.1 shows the long-term trend of intended durations in tax-farming contracts. The contract duration statistics, spanning from 1535 to 1800, indicate an S-shaped pattern that may result from the effects of institutional change due to the exogenous shocks and endogenous dynamics.

Figure 6.2 presents the intended durations of contracts constructed from primary sources (See for example, Çizakça, 1993; Genç, 2000). The data presented in Fig. 6.2 indicates average intended durations for 24-year periods. The limitations of data allow to establish such periodization. As given above, the tax-farming contracts include limited duration from one year to 12 years. However, the average values have indicated that 12-year

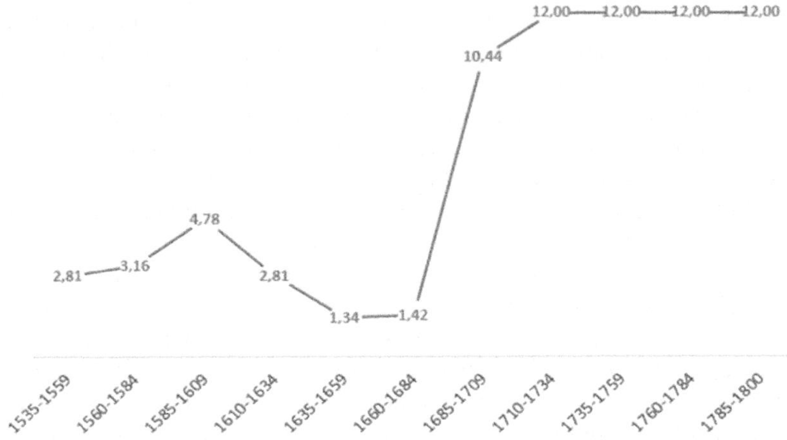


**Fig. 6.1** The long-term trend of intended durations of tax-farming contracts

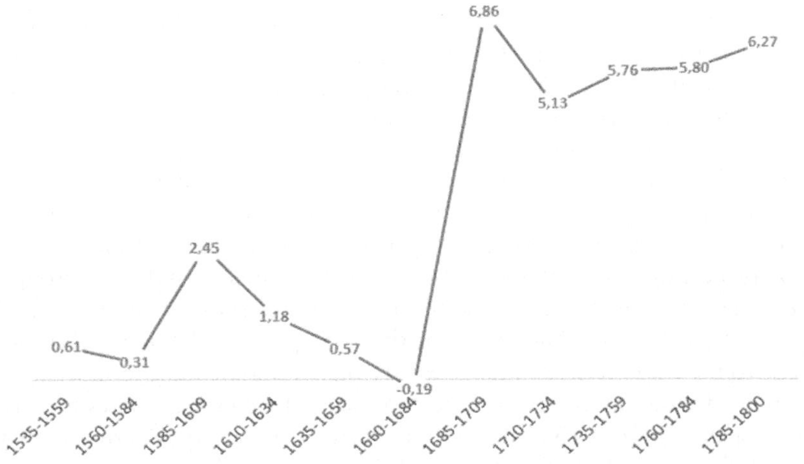


**Fig. 6.2** The long-term trend of difference between intended and actual durations

contracts were at the modest levels. One of the most important issues is the jump in average values from 1.42 to 10.44. The main reason is that the central authority changed the rules of the game toward lifetime tax-farming contracts in the last years of the seventeenth century. Although lifetime contracts included limited information about how much time the agents held the contracts, the advance payments (*muaccele*) indicate an approximate period about the intended durations. The historical background has argued that the central authority determined this advance payment regarding 10 to 12 times of annual payments. This indicates that it was expected that the agents would hold the contracts for 10–12 years. Thus, the intended durations are considered 12 years as is shown in Fig. 6.2.

During the sixteenth century, the intended durations had an increasing pattern in which contracts were arranged with 3–5 years. The central authority imposed relatively longer contract durations regarding 1-year contracts. The nature of tax-farming contracts, however, limited contracting parties to expand contract durations for longer terms. The intended contract durations indicated approximately an inverted U-Shaped pattern for a century between 1535 and 1635. The domination of short-term contracts entailed losses in state revenues during the same period (Fig. 6.1). More importantly, budget deficits emerged with an increasing pattern until the middle of the seventeenth century. The central authority imposed longer-duration contracts by changing the rules of the game. The change, however, was selective and emerged in contract durations. This caused a jump in intended durations from the beginning of the seventeenth century (Fig. 6.2). The problem was that this limited change within the rules of the game was adequate to change the perception of agents in contractual relations.

Figure 6.3 shows the average differences between intended and actual contract durations in the Ottoman Empire. The intended durations reflected changing rules within the institutional structure. The difference, however, emerged from changing perception of agents. Until the last decades of the seventeenth century, the differences seemed low because of short-term contracts. The emergence of lifetime tax-farming contracts caused increases in intended durations from the eighteenth century. The differences jumped during the last years of the seventeenth century. This probably resulted from the fact that lifetime tax-farming contracts increased the intended durations. As Fig. 6.3 indicated that the contracts were terminated approximately halfway through the intended duration. As given in historical background, changes in rules were selective and increases in contract durations failed to solve problems in

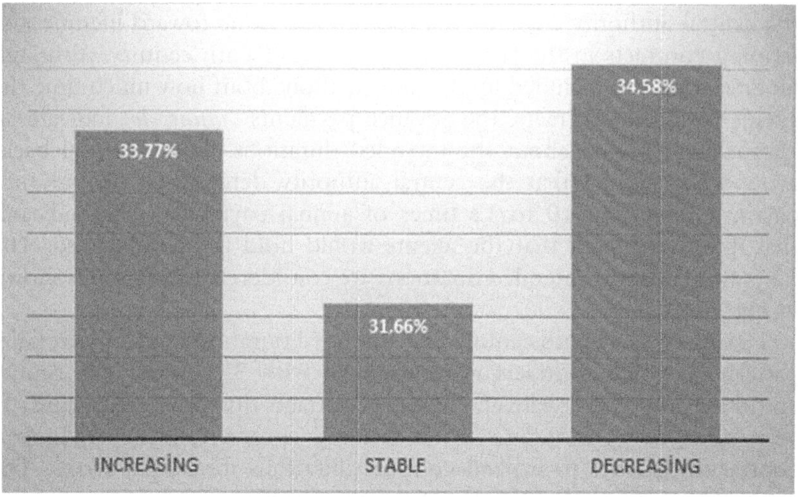


**Fig. 6.3** The allocation of contracts by price changes in auctions

law enforcement. In other words, the domination of interest groups—judicial/religious-based agents—limited institutional change during the eighteenth century.

The central authority continued to assign judicial agents, and courts maintained their dependence on the central authority. The failure to the establishment of private and independent courts entailed commitment problems in contractual relations. The judicial/religious-based agents as powerful groups within the institutional environment had a strong incentive to protect their interests in the existing structure. These groups of agents could gain higher revenues in court approvals during auctions. Meanwhile, they had the power to manipulate contracting parties to behave in favor of their interests. Once a local court reported opportunistic behavior against an agent, the central authority could easily transfer existing contracts toward new groups thanks to its absolute power. The opportunistic behavior reported by judicial/religious-based agents did not have to be based on real actions, fabricated allegations could be adequate to change the perception of the central authority. In this sense, judicial/religious-based agents had the chance to increase their interests by forcing agents to establish partnerships with them. Thus, the differences presented in Fig. 6.3 were based not only on pure opportunistic behaviors of contracting parties but also on actions taken by judicial/religious-based agents during the eighteenth century.

The second important indicator in examining the rule of law within the institutional structure was changing prices in tax-farming and life-time tax-farming contracts over time. The importance of prices emerged from the legal structure of the Ottoman Empire. The law enforcement and judicial decisions had different effects in changing the prices of contracts. The price changes also determined strategies and actions taken by contracting parties during the early modern period. As it was given in contract durations, the central authority chose to re-allocate tax-farming contracts toward new agents. The long-term trend of difference between intended and actual durations showed that the allocation of contracts was based on two different causes. The first cause emerged from exogenous shocks. Once a shock emerged, the central authority chose to use its coercive power to terminate existing contracts. By doing this way, the central authority re-auctioned these contracts with higher prices to increase its revenues.

Secondly, structural changes in the central authority caused shifts in the balance of power between powerful groups located in Istanbul. Once a new group started to dominate the political structure, they chose to terminate existing contracts and allocate them toward their agents located in provinces. In other words, different agents and provincial notables could capture economic and political privileges through tax-farming contracts.

The price changes in contracts, however, provided information on the reasons behind changing contractual relations. Regardless of the basic principles of the rule of law, contracts could not be terminated unilaterally. Even if this happened, the legal structure should make sure that the loss of the injured party had to be compensated within the economic environment. Otherwise, it was difficult to argue over an effective legal structure. The judicial decision, in this sense, played a crucial role in this process. Their partnerships with coercive power limited the ability of injured parties to limit the power of the central authority. Within the Ottoman case, judicial/religious-based agents sided with the central authority to protect their interests. In an institutional structure where judicial/religious-based agents were appointed by the central authority, this was an understandable strategy. The problem was why did the

Ottoman Empire fail to establish an institutional structure supporting independent courts and judges?

The dataset established included annual prices committed by the agents. These prices and their trends provided explicit evidence of the effects of institutional failures in the Ottoman Empire. As it was shown above, the substantial part of tax-farming contracts changed hands before their intended durations. This emerged from weak law enforcement due to the strategic positions of judicial/religious-based agents within the institutional environment. The price levels of contracts showed that the contractual relationships were based on political relations. The main purpose of the central authority was to maximize state revenues. The auction mechanism emerged as an institution tool to achieve this goal. The data based on primary sources presented that the prices of about 35% of the contracts had decreased. Meanwhile, 32% of contracts stayed at the same price during the auctions. The failure in prices offered by the agents had three main sources. First, wealth-maximizing agents recognized depreciation in financial resources due to the exploitation of former agents. Secondly, agents had the political power to obtain tax-farming contracts with lower prices. Thirdly, the opportunistic behavior of the central authority emerged as a convention, and this caused changes in the perception of agents. Thus, agents had an incentive to offer lower prices for a contract.

## Causes and Consequences: Interactions Among Contracting Parties

Under positive transaction costs, uncertainty shapes the perception of agents (North, 1990). Changing institutions toward more efficient ones could create inefficient outcomes due to the perception of players who gained from the current situation. Some of the tax-farming contracts that were extracted from archives bore such situations out. In one case, the State and agents had 13 agreements on the "Ports of Anatolia" under the tax-farming institution between 1589 and 1621. While the intended duration of these contracts was six years on average, contracts usually ended in 2.5 years. Furthermore, the annual prices of these contracts that were determined under auction increased from 194.000 *akches* to 244.000 *akches*.[1]

As shown above, each agent could make an offer for a contract even if this contract was current. If the agent committed to matching the amount of a new offer by a rival, the State and the current agent reestablished the contract under new terms. Otherwise, the State transferred the contract toward the new bidder. For instance, "Salonica Customs" changed hands three times in a year during 1596. Each contract had six years, but conditions of the first two contracts had changed in less than one year because of new higher offers by rival agents. In the third offer, a new agent obtained tax collecting rights of Salonica customs for six years. The final agent, however, could only hold rights for four years.[2] While a six-year contract was changing hands three times in a year, annual prices committed by agents also fluctuated from 1.56 million to 1.83 million *akches*, and finally to 1.45 million *akches*.[3] This situation reflected the agent's strategies. On the one hand, agents could increase annual prices by offering higher bids to increase the current agent's costs. On the other hand, agents could influence high-ranking bureaucrats by offering a share from contracts to obtain tax-farming rights at lower prices. In addition to agents, the State could act opportunistically by confiscating contracts with its coercive power, particularly in war periods and in times of major changes in the State, such as the replacement of sultans or high-ranking bureaucrats.

The existing literature argues that tax-collecting agents would improve productivity more than salaried government officials. Since agents bore all risks on lands under tax-farming contracts, they were expected to increase returns from contracts with minimum costs (Darling, 1996, p. 119). Thus, the competition between agents would bring higher revenues for the central treasure. During this period, while the competition was raising the values of contracts and revenues of the central budget, price increases

[1] The Contracts of Ports of Anatolia, MAD 2477/50 MAD 2477/77 MAD 2477/87 MAD 2477/105 MAD 2477/107 MAD 2477/128 MAD 598/4 MAD 3360/54 MAD 3360/63 MAD 357/89 MAD 2957/85. For more information about a competitive structure on these contracts, see Çizakça (1993).

[2] There was a lack of data in primary sources because the six-years arrangement ended at the end of the fourth year.

[3] MAD, 2477/47; MAD, 624/1; MAD, 2477/122; MAD, 2477/136, see also Çizakça (1993).

started to diminish. The stagnation in prices led to a dominant equilibrium in the institutional structure.[4] Decreasing prices on tax-farming contracts due to the dominant strategy (defections) were compatible with decreases in both budget revenues and per capita tax revenues (Table 4.1). During the same period, the Ottoman Empire started to lag behind Western European societies (Table 4.2). The rules of the game and incentive mechanisms indicated that reneging on contracts for each party was the dominant strategy in the short run, encouraged by the relatively free entrance to the market to offer a new price and the coercive power of the State.

While exogenous influences were prominent on the process of institutional change, the direction of institutional change and economic performance of the empire was mainly determined by endogenous dynamics that emerged from transactions between the State and its agents. Societies that solved endogenous problems seem to have fared better in economic development. North and Weingast (1989) examined how England solved endogenous problems that emerged under the rules of the game related to relations between the ruler and agents regarding property rights and state borrowing perspective. According to the study, the problem of cooperation was solved by restricting the power of the ruler to honor its obligations.

In the same way, Hilton Root (1989) argued that the corporate bodies established by elites became efficient to limit the coercive power of the State. Balla and Jonhson (2009) presented a comparative perspective between tax-farming mechanisms of the Ottoman Empire and France. This study argues that there was a lack of corporate bodies established by powerful groups in the Ottoman Empire. This argument was also available in the existing literature for the contractual relations in the Ottoman Empire except for Halil İnalcık (1994) and Mehmet Genç (2000). Yet, the existing literature had a deficiency in giving a theoretical explanation of why agents failed to establish corporate bodies in the Ottoman Empire.

[4] For instance, annual payments of "Aleppo Bac-i Siyah" contracts decreased from 63 to 29 kg of silver between 1581 and 1609. Another important tax-farming contracts' price decreased from 83 to 55 kg of silver between 1595 and 1621. The prices of "Damascus Taxes" contracts sharply decreased from 196 to 74 kg of silver between 1561 and 1636. These examples could be augmented for not only tax collecting rights of markets but also ports and industrial organizations. MAD 4972/114, 116, 117, 118, 120; MAD 2706/14; MAD 919/8; MAD 5604/25; MAD 4383/71, 737; MAD 657/80. For the competitive structure of these tax-farming contracts, see Çizakça (1993).

As given above, historical evidence shows that the dominant strategy of the State was to have the contract. Asymmetric information and uncertainty determined the strategic behaviors of the players toward defection. Figure 6.3 presented differences between the intended and actual duration of tax-farming contracts. In other words, this figure showed increasing coordination and commitment problems under the tax-farming institution from the beginning of the sixteenth century to the end of the eighteenth century. The auction mechanism and committed payments created incentives for opportunistic behavior and diverted resources to different goals. Agents had to pay the auction price rather than investing in lands. As their costs increased with the increasing density of auctions, agents had to decide to get a contract with a payment or not to get a contract. If there were payments to obtain a contract, then the investment would be lower.

On the other side, the state preferred to act opportunistically when it faced shocks. Wars increased expenses in addition to keeping a regular army as in other European societies. As war expenses increased, the central budget needed more financial resources (Karaman & Pamuk, 2010, p. 596). The State, however, employed tax-farming contracts as domestic borrowing mechanisms that helped to collect future taxes in advance (Pamuk, 2004, p. 240; Pamuk, 2009, p. 22; Karaman & Pamuk, 2010, p. 598). However, the State confiscated contracts before their intended duration ends and had new auctions with higher prices (Fig. 6.3).

In sum, the State confiscated contracts because of rivalry between agents. In particular, the State preferred to cooperate with agents who committed to making higher payments and provided soldiers for campaigns in times of crisis. It took advantage of its coercive power to confiscate contracts for economic gains. The State could also confiscate contracts due to the complaints by local people, according to court rulings. These complaints could emerge from rival agents who paid bribes to local people to file complaints about the current agent. To sum up, the coercive power and complaints from local people were the main determinants of the confiscation strategy of the State in addition to exogenous shocks such as wars.

Possible strategies of the State and its agents are summarized below (Table 6.1), using primary resources and historical literature. Each strategy shows how the State and agents deviate from the rules. By deviating from the rules, each player created economic returns on their behalf in the short term.

**Table 6.1** Defection strategies under tax-farming contracts

| *The State* | *Agents* |
|---|---|
| - Seize tax-farming contracts without any costs | - Crop more share from tax revenues |
| - Transfer tax-farming rights toward higher bidders without any cost | - Create asymmetric information. Agents could deviate by exploiting lands while decreased the future expected value of lands |
| - Increase costs of agents by utilizing complaints | - Politically powerful agents could assign their agents as state officials into monitoring mechanisms to increase costs of the State such as information, punishment costs |

How would the State and its agents honor their commitments in the institutional structure? There were also sub-problems, such as why players acted only reactively to others' choices? Why repeatedly interacting generations of each party could not guess the other party's risk preferences correctly, or did they? Why could the bounded rational players not perfectly foresee the consequence of collective actions? We try to find answers to these questions in the following section.

**Acknowledgements** MAD represents specific records of Ottoman Archives in which tax-farming contracts are classified.

## References

### Primary Sources

MAD 2477/50; MAD 2477/77; MAD 2477/87; MAD 2477/105; MAD 2477/107; MAD 2477/128; MAD 598/4; MAD 3360/54; MAD 3360/63; MAD 357/89; MAD 2957/85; MAD, 2477/47; MAD, 624/1; MAD, 2477/122; MAD, 2477/136; MAD 4972/114, 116, 117, 118, 120; MAD 2706/14; MAD 919/8; MAD 5604/25; MAD 4383/71, 737; MAD 657/80.

## Secondary Sources


Balla, E., & Johnson, N. D. (2009). Fiscal crisis and institutional change in the Ottoman Empire and France. *The Journal of Economic History, 69*(3), 809–845.

Çizakça, M. (1993). Tax-farming and financial decentralization in the Ottoman economy: 1520–1697. *The Journal of European Economic History, 22*(2), 219–250.

Darling, L. (1996). *Revenue-raising and legitimacy: Tax collecting and finance administration in the Ottoman Empire, 1560–1660*. E. J. Brill.

Genç, M. (2000). *Osmanlı İmparatorluğu'nda Devlet ve Ekonomi*. Ötüken Neşriyat.

İnalcik, H. (1994). *An economic and social history of the Ottoman Empire, 1300–1914*. Cambridge University Press.

Karaman, K. K., & Pamuk, Ş. (2010). Ottoman state finances in European perspective. *The Journal of Economic History, 70*(3), 593–629.

North, D. C. (1990). *Institutions, institutional change and economic performance*. Cambridge University Press.

North, D. C., & Weingast, B. R. (1989). Constitutions and commitment: The evolution of institutions governing public choice in seventeenth century England. *The Journal of Economic History, 49*(4), 803–832.

Pamuk, Ş. (2004). Institutional change and the longevity of the Ottoman Empire, 1500–1800. *The Journal of Interdisciplinary History, 35*(2), 225–247.

Pamuk, Ş. (2009). Changes in factor markets in the Ottoman Empire 1500–1800. *Continuity and Change, 24*(1), 1–30.

Root, H. L. (1989). Tying the king's hands: Credible commitment and royal fiscal policy during the old regime. *Rationality and Society, 1*(2), 240–258.

CHAPTER 7

# Prisoner's Dilemma as a Tool to Analyze Tax-Farming Institutions

**Abstract** This chapter gives a game-theoretical model of tax-farming contracts to examine the level of the rule of law in the Ottoman Empire. We employ tools from Prisoner's Dilemma game for two reasons. First, the PD game is a simple embodiment of establishing cooperation in contractual relations. In this sense, the PD game generates the basis of our theoretical perspective to analyze equilibrium(s) and outcome(s) as well as the rule of law. Secondly, the assumptions of the PD game are compatible with the payoffs proposed from primary sources based on tax-farming contracts and court records. The game-theoretical model has suggested that once a contractual arrangement emerged between the central authority and the agent, the strategies of contracting parties were mostly defection. Thus, a Nash Equilibrium(s) has emerged within the institutional environment. Game theory has argued that Nash equilibrium(s) is Pareto inferior, and the Pareto optimum outcomes are based on cooperation among contracting parties. The main reason is that selective and partial institutional change entailed failure to establish a competitive structure within the institutional environment. The structure of law and the role of judicial/religious-based agents had limited the institutional change to protect their interests in contractual relations. In terms of the rule of law, this study has argued that the Ottoman Empire became a typical example of a "limited access order". The structure of law and its judges, however, had prevented agents from developing



B. Altay and F. Oğuz, *Rules, Contracts and Law Enforcement in the Ottoman Empire*, Palgrave Studies in Institutions, Economics and Law, https://doi.org/10.1007/978-3-030-79577-1_7

mechanisms in limiting the coercive power of the central authority. The judicial/religious-based agents had used their influence to maintain the institutional structure as it did.

**Keywords** The Ottoman Empire · Tax-farming contracts · Prisoner's dilemma · Nash equilibrium · Judicial decisions

The tax-farming system was used extensively throughout history. Almost all societies, Western European Countries, Low Countries, and some of Middle East Countries used various tax-collecting mechanisms to defray wars and states (Darling, 1996, p. 122; Ma & Rubin, 2019; Root, 1989; van Bavel, 2015, p. 76).

In this system, elites or high-ranking bureaucrats acquired certain economic and political rights from the State in return for tax payments (Salzmann, 1993, p. 400). The State could collect taxes through the hands of elites before production, and tax farmers gained a profit from the difference between the total revenue and the committed tax payment. This mechanism differed from country to country, and the Ottoman Empire developed an institutional structure by employing tax-farming contracts. These contracts provided rights that were allocated to agents and provincial notables through the auction mechanism. The State signed a contract with an agent who committed to pay the highest price (Çizakça, 1996, p. 140; Darling, 1996, p. 119; Kuran, 2005, p. 824; Pamuk, 2009, p. 22; Salzmann, 2004, p. 113). As given in historical background, the new institutional structure caused shifts in coalitions and alliances (Karaman & Pamuk, 2010, p. 597; Pamuk, 2004b, pp. 236–239; Pamuk, 2009, p. 2; Yaycioglu, 2016). Provincial notables started to dominate the contract market by establishing collusion with judicial/religious-based agents within the institutional structures. Within the contractual relations, the returns would be higher for each contracting party if productivity could be increased through incentives. In sum, the rules were given under the decentralized institution. The rules are given as follows.

- The State transferred tax-farming rights toward agents, who offered the highest price for a contract.

- Each agent did a cost–benefit analysis to offer an efficient price within the auction mechanism.
- The State and its agents made a contractual arrangement between one and 12 years.
- Each agent had to pay committed tax to the State at the end of the first year.
- If the State received a higher offer from another agent, the State could transfer tax-farming rights through its absolute power to a new agent (No corporate body to limit absolute power). If the former agent committed to pay the price of the new offer, the State renewed the contract with the former agent regarding the new price.
- If an agent reneged on a contract, this agent would lose tax-farming rights with a specific punishment by the State.

Before constructing the dichotomy of the central authority and agents, it should be noted that the game is based on tax-farming contracts instead of lifetime tax-farming contracts. This is because of a fundamental difference in the rules of the game. Tax-farming contracts are mostly based on commitments of the agents. Auctions determine the prices of contracts and each agent is responsible for transferring committed annual payments at the end of the first year or period. Under the lifetime tax-farming contracts, however, agents have to pay an advance payment called *muaccele*. The rules of the game have changed with this advance payment. As it is discussed above, tax-farming contracts dominated the institutional structure for a longer period. Furthermore, including advance payment into the game makes the structure more complex and comprehensive. Instead, the main purpose of this study is to present a simple version of contractual relations. For this reason, the game presented in this study focused on a game that played only one period. This specific model should be sufficient to present the essence of contractual relations within the institutional environment. More importantly, the main purpose of this first attempt to create a game-theoretic model of tax-farming contracts is to contribute to the ongoing debates on Ottoman revenue-extracting institutions with a new discussion. To achieve this goal, the game excludes lifetime tax-farming contracts, which included advance payments in obtaining economic and political privileges under the institutional structure.

Demonstrating an analytical and systematic analysis of equilibrium(s) emerged in contractual relations before discussing the role of the legal

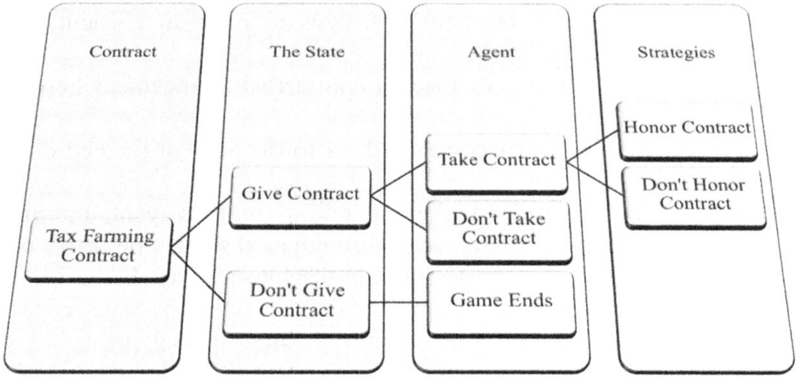


**Fig. 7.1** The structure of contract relation

structure provides a better understanding of the role of the legal structure. Figure 7.1 gives the game tree that presents the stages toward the emergence of a tax-farming contract.

The state had the power to contract a financial resource or not in the Ottoman Empire. In other words, the State could extract revenues from a financial resource by employing either state officials or agents. If the State decided not to give a contract, this meant state officials were responsible for tax-collecting, and the game would end. When the State decided to give a contract under the auction mechanism, the game would continue with choices of agents whether "take contract" or "do not take contract".

The structure of agents, under the tax-farming institution, also changed with the new rules of the game. The former agents in the timar institution were mostly military-based individuals, and they could obtain contracts regarding their achievements during campaigns. The military agents had a lower chance to choose their contracts by calculating costs and benefits of the land they were willing to obtain. The changing structure of agents enabled them to choose their contracts to maximize their gains from contractual arrangements. If an agent offered the highest price to take the contract, the game would continue, or vice versa.

Once the game started between the State and its agents, the State determined the contract duration between one to 12 years (Çizakça, 1993, p. 233–250; Darling, 1996, p. 135; Karaman & Pamuk, 2010, p. 601; Pamuk, 2004a, p. 16; 2004b, p. 240; Salzmann, 1993, p. 339). Each year represented periods of the game. In other words, tax-farming

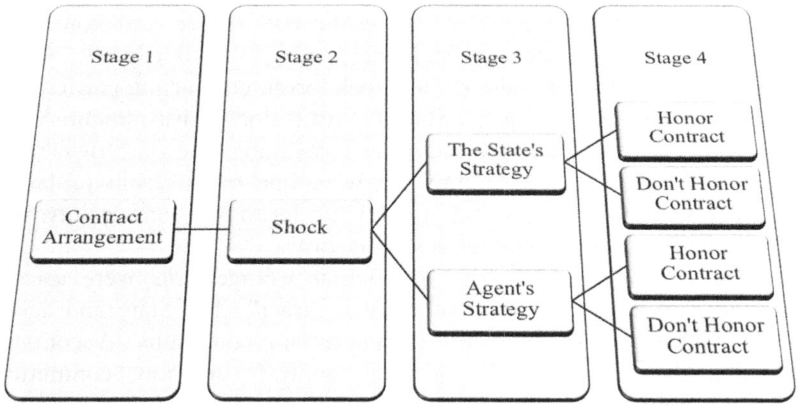


**Fig. 7.2** The stages of game play

contracts had 12 periods at most, where $t_i$ represented each period within the institutional structure. The "contract" stage was the beginning of a tax-farming contract, $t_0$.

At time $t_0$, the State put up a tax-farming contract for auction to capture tax revenues. In the "State" stage, the State decided to give the contract or not. At the same time, the "agent" stage emerged where agents decided to take a contract or not but offering prices for a tax-farming contract. Both archival documents and historical studies showed that agents had strong incentives to obtain tax-farming contracts from the State (Barkey, 2008; Çizakça, 1993; Darling, 1996; Salzmann, 2004; Yaycioglu, 2016). The salaried state officials worked in the finance department of the central authority increased from 35 to 188 between 1535 and 1645. This provides an important evidence for increasing the tax base of the Ottoman Empire with the new institutional structure (Darling, 1996, p. 45). Thus, the dominant strategy of both the State and its agents was to establish contractual relations: "take contract". From this equilibrium, the game continued under the strategies of the contracting period. The game form and payoffs reflected the periods of "take contract" and "end of the actual duration".

Figure 7.2 shows the stages of the game played after a tax-farming contract established between the State and its agents. Stage 1 represents the equilibrium of "take contract" in which the State and agents formally started contractual relations under court approval. Once an agent received *Berat* from the judge, the game had started and continued toward the stages where the strategies emerge. At one point of the game, an exogenous or endogenous shock forced contracting parties, and hence, the strategies emerged within the institutional environment (Stage 2). Contracts were made for the short term under the state ownership on lands. While short-term contracts were one of the main problems of profit-seeking activities and investment incentives, uncertainty was another major problem in contractual relations.

As shown in Fig. 7.1, the contractual arrangements were usually concluded at the equilibrium of "take contract". The State and agent made contractual arrangements under certain conditions. A contract included the agent's name and title, contract duration, committed payment amounts of agents, court approval (*berat*), and also expected revenues of agents from arrangements. Figure 7.2 gives an outline of how the game was played. Some sorts of shocks, however, could emerge due to the changing conditions. Emerging shocks created new incentive mechanisms for contracting parties to form new strategies to increase individual gains at the end of actual duration. Strategies would shape the structure of the game and the outcomes of contracts. In other words, strategies would determine the equilibrium (s) that affected the economic performance of the Ottoman Empire in the long run instead of short-run gains (Tables 4.1 and 4.2).

To understand how institutional mechanisms were working and what mechanisms emerged as the solution of problems, the dominant strategies and equilibrium(s) have to be stated. Archival evidence points out two critical issues under the rules of the game. As it is mentioned in the historical background, the State had a coercive power all over the empire, and agents, particularly unemployed agents, could make a new offer for a contract, even this contract was arranged very recently. These two rules shaped incentive mechanisms of contracting parties to change strategies. Thus, the third stage of the game was formed according to the incentive mechanisms that emerged from the rules of the game at the end of the actual duration.

The direction of strategies of contracting parties could be observed from contracts for the third stage. Once a shock was discovered, the State could seize the contract to increase its revenues by reallocating contracts with a new auction toward agents. According to Kütahya Court Records, the State transferred tax-farming rights of "Tavşanlı and Geyikli *Bac* Taxes" from Miroğlu to Turdanoğlu Mehmed, who might offer a higher price for the contract. The court register that the justified assignment of Turdanoğlu Mehmed included any price about the contract (KŞS II, 102/510). On the other side, agents tried to keep gains from contracts at higher levels by pursuing rent-seeking activities. If confiscation expectations on contracts were high for agents, the dominant strategy would be to defect on the contract. Defection took many forms. One of the most interesting defections on contracts by agents was to produce goods that provided higher gains and destruction on the soil in the short run. As Yuzo Nagata (1999) indicated, the State limited production of goods such as cotton and rice on lands subjected to tax-farming contracts.

Powerful local groups, however, preferred to create incentives to produce cotton instead of committed conditions on contracts. In other words, destructive use on lands started to be a prevalent or dominant strategy for agents. By producing more cotton, both the productivity of lands and the production of staple goods decreased. While agents increased revenues from lands with cotton production, the value of lands subjected to tax-farming contracts fell along with productivity. In addition to production problems, agents pressured producers by creating extra payments in addition to statutory tax rates to collect more tax revenues. In Kutahya Province, the governor and other smaller political actors (*voivodes*) dominated tax-farming rights, and their secondary agents, who were responsible to collect taxes on behalf of primary agents, forced taxpayers to pay extra amounts in 1698 (Kütahya Court Records, KŞS II, 102/510).

The defaulting strategies of agents could be followed by specific documents about court judgments. These judgments mostly included producers' complaints about agents. For instance, there was a court judgment to prevent taxpayers from abusing the behaviors of agents, who consisted of *sancakbey* of Çirmen and his agents during the 1580s. Besides, these groups of agents forced individuals who were exempt from taxes (Çirmen Court Records, ÇŞS 15, 80;100). After judgments reached to the State, tax-farming contracts could be terminated or seized by the State to transfer them to another agent with a new auction. The judgments about the existing agent could be created by competitor agents and their local representatives. The third stage of the game included major information problems, asymmetric information, and moral hazard problems. First, information was costly for contracting parties.

Second, agents hired local agents from powerful and wealthier local groups. While agents preferred to stay close to the State, their local representatives managed tax-farming contracts (Pamuk, 2009, p. 23). Local representatives had better knowledge about their provinces. Thus, cheating emerged as a possibility. The agents, Rıdvan and Ahmed, paid only 35.000 akches as tax revenue. But after an investigation, these agents crop higher shares from tax revenues instead of paying 89.500 akches more to the central budget during the 1580s (ÇŞS 15, 103–104). Similar opportunistic behavior that cropping higher shares from tax revenues continued even in the first decades of the nineteenth century. A court record showed that agents cropped higher shares and send fewer tax revenues than committed payments (TŞS 50, 7/18).

One of the most important mechanisms to keep local representatives honest was to grant titles to them. Thus, transaction costs were growing for the State from not only asymmetric information and moral hazard but also increasing numbers of intermediaries in provinces. Increasing numbers of agents emerged from not only higher demands of agents but also employed secondary agents, who were employed by primary agents. Once new agents obtained a tax-farming contract, they eliminated secondary agents of former agents and employed their agents. Each secondary agent became a sharecropper. According to Kütahya court records, Mustafa Pasha, who obtained tax-farming rights of former agent Abdi Pasha, assigned Eyyup Agha and Veli Agha as his secondary agents in collecting taxes (KŞS II, 86/447) In Bolu court records, Yusuf Pasha, the primary agent, collected approximately 8.000 qurushes with the hands of his secondary agents. One of these agents was a state officer (*müteselsim*), who had the authority to govern and monitor certain territories (BŞS 836, 32; 85). Governance of these provinces started to be costly, and favoritism became dominant under the existing rules of the game.

High-ranking bureaucrats who were also agents served indefinite periods that were depended on the duration of the Sultan's reign. When the Sultan was replaced, high-ranking bureaucrats also lost their political positions. As a result, local representatives of the agents, both provincial notables and judicial/religious-based agents, also lost their contractual rights. In other words, strong relations between agents and their local representatives determined which groups would have contracts. High-ranking bureaucrats gained economic power from these contracts, but local groups gained not only economic revenues but also political titles and high-ranking status according to the conditions of contracts. New political titles and duties started to be attached to contract terms. The third stage of the game gave way to the fourth stage. If the State reneged

**Table 7.1** Key variables

| | | | |
|---|---|---|---|
| $C$ | Numbers of contracts | $K$ | State's revenue without a contract |
| $A$ | Numbers of agents | $R$ | Agent's reservation utility |
| $\Pi^e$ | State's revenue under a contract | $\lambda_1, \lambda_2$ | Gains from mutual defection |
| $T^e$ | Agent's revenue under a contract | $S_A$ | Agent's gain when the state cheated |
| $L^e$ | Total wealth from a contract | $S_S$ | State's gain when agent cheated |
| $\alpha$ | Agent's gain from cheating | $\phi$ | State's gain from opportunistic behavior |

first, then the agent's strategy would be reneging on contracts or vice versa. The main problem was reneging strategy emerged as a dominant strategy for each party.

For the fourth stage, a model facilitates the examination of the institutional structure and its contract-enforcement mechanisms in an economy from a specific period of history. This model is based on Prisoner's Dilemma when the strategies and historical evidence presented in previous chapters are considered. The game played in the fourth stage is a Prisoner's Dilemma because the rules of the game and legal structure direct contracting parties to opportunistic behavior. If contracting parties choose defection, they can gain higher payoffs (Bowles, 2004) (Table 7.1).

Within the institutional environment, the State had contracts up to C, and the number of agents was A, where A is higher than C (A > C). This equation showed why the Ottoman Empire employed an auction mechanism in the allocation of tax-farming contracts for almost three hundred years. Whatever the transaction costs (asymmetric information or moral hazard) according to the types of agents in employing for auction mechanism by the State, the auction mechanism was the dominant strategy of the State at time $t_0$. In other words, there was a possibility for employing deceptive agents by the State as long as they offered the highest price during auctions. Players lived infinite numbers of the period, and $b$ is the discount factor of the agents. Besides, unemployed agents had a reservation utility per period of $R > 0$. In each period, an agent could obtain only one contract from the State by offering the highest price, and each agent randomly offered a price for a contract for different territories of

| | | The State | |
|---|---|---|---|
| | | Cooperate | Defect |
| Agents | Invest | $\Pi^e, T^e$ | $S_A, \phi$ |
| | Not Invest | $\alpha, S_S$ | $\lambda_1, \lambda_2$ |

**Fig. 7.3** The payoffs of tax-farming contracts at the end of the actual duration

the Ottoman Empire. If the State preferred not to give a contract to an agent, it received a payoff $K$, where $K > 0$.

On the other hand, if the State made a contract with the agent, the shares of the agent and the State were determined regarding the highest offer. The highest offer by an agent was $T_e$, which was also the total expected tax revenue of the State at the end of the $t_1$. The agents' gain was $\Pi^e$ total expected profit of the agent at the end of the $t_1$. It was assumed that the total expected tax revenues of the State were higher than its reservation utility, $T_e > K$. In this sense, the agents' total expected gains from tax-farming contracts were also higher than their reservation utility, $\Pi^e > R$. At this point, an agent chose to be honest or a cheater. If the agent preferred, to be honest, the State could gain $Te$, and the agent could gain $\Pi^e$. Hence, the total gain from cooperation was $L_e$, where $L_e = T_e + \Pi^e$. In other words, $L_e$ was the total wealth that was created from a tax-farming contract. Furthermore, it was assumed that cooperation emerges as long as $Le$ remained bigger than $K + R$ (form a contract was efficient).

Figure 7.3 presents the payoff table that emerged from the contractual relationship between the State and its agents. In a game-theoretical perspective, the best strategies of contracting parties and their responses to each other's strategies are given as follows:

$\lambda_2 > S_S$; If the agent chose "not to invest" in a financial resource subjected to a tax-farming contract, the best response of the State would be defection. If the State chose to cooperate under this assumption, it would face three different losses of gain. First, a financial resource without investment would lose its productivity in the long term. When the State put this contract on a new auction, there would be lower offers with the lower price due to the decreasing productivity. The changing structure of agents under the tax-farming contracts had the right to choose contracts they offered. As a wealth-maximizer individual, each agent should make their profit/loss analysis before giving an offer in auctions. Secondly, agents could force producers for cultivating products that provided higher gains in the short term but decreased productivity of financial resources in the long term. This caused decreases in the value of the financial resources. Finally, when agents were perceived that monitoring mechanisms were ineffective or that they had the power to bypass them, they would choose to allocate a higher share to them from the revenues, again causing loss of earnings against the State. The final strategy of agents was directly related to the role of judicial/religious-based agents within the legal structure. The *kadis* (highest judges) formed the monitoring mechanisms, and they were responsible for preventing agents from opportunistic behaviors within the contractual relations.

$S_S > T_e$; If the agent chose to invest in a financial resource, the best response of the State would be defection within the game. An investment made by the agent caused emerging free-rider problems within the institutional environment. First, once an agent invested in a financial resource within the tax-farming institution, rival agents would offer higher prices to the State to obtain this financial resource. A price offered lower than the investment costs of the former agent allowed the new agent to capture gains of investment made by the former agent. As historical evidence showed that the State had the right to transfer contracts toward new agents once it received a higher price. Thus, the State had the chance to increase its revenues through the investment of former agents.

$\phi > T^e$; If the State chose to cooperate (honor contract until the end of the intended duration), the best response of agents would be "not to invest". The tax-farming contracts were established for short terms in which the agents would find the "not to invest" strategy beneficial within the game.

$\alpha > \Pi^e$; If the State chose defection as the best strategy, the revenues would be increased while agents faced a loss of gain at the end of the actual duration. If the agent followed cooperation within the contractual relationship, this agent suffered from the loss because of investing in financial resources in the short term. Thus, the agent would get *SA*, which was lower than *ll*.

Finally, the question of why the payoffs of cooperation (invest, cooperate) would be higher than those that emerged in mutual defection (not to invest, defection) should be explained for the institutional environment that emerged in the Ottoman Empire. Two relations among variables should be sufficient to examine this question within the rules of the game.

$\Pi^e > \lambda_1$ and $T^e > \lambda_2$; An agent, who decided to invest in a financial resource within a contractual relation, would increase revenues if the State honor the contract until the end of the intended duration. This agent was able to enjoy higher returns because of increasing productivity and efficiency in financial resources. Furthermore, once the contract duration ended regarding the intended duration, the agent had a strong incentive to offer a higher price to the State to protect the investment made before. This probably results from the fact that leaving the contract will cause economic loss, and hence, the agent would offer a higher price to the State. The emergence of this result depended on the perception of agents about strategies of the State. If the agents believed that the State would honor contracts no matter what shocks occurred within the economic and political environment. Similarly, a credible commitment made by the State would create incentive mechanisms for the agents to invest financial resources in both short-term and long-term contracts.

These variables and their relations among each other are compatible with the historical background as well as presented information through primary sources. The game theory allows us to simplify contractual relations that emerged in the Ottoman Empire during the early modern period. As it is given in Fig. 7.3, each party had two strategies: cooperation or defection. The theoretical background (Prisoner's Dilemma) indicates that mutual defection was the equilibrium within the institutional structure of the Ottoman Empire. However, this equilibrium is Pareto inferior. This means the institutional environment of the Ottoman Empire contained different equilibrium(s) that promoted Pareto optimum outcomes.

The question of why the Ottoman Empire had failed to establish more beneficial outcomes within the institutional structure becomes an important and complicated issue in examining the economic performance of the Ottoman Empire. The game-theoretical perspective provides evidence about why inefficient outcomes emerged within the institutional structure. The variables presented in payoff tables, however, are based mostly on economic institutions that contained rules in contracts. The role of legal structure and perception of judicial/religious-based agents should be included in the analysis.

The differences between intended and actual durations were important evidence of weak law enforcement in the Ottoman Empire. On the one hand, the State achieved to protect its coercive power through judicial/religious-based agents. The Ottoman courts took the authority and power from the State. The highest judges were assigned by the State. These groups of agents enjoyed gains from a judicial decision, and more importantly, if the tax-farming contracts were allocated through courts, judges could increase their gains. Furthermore, these judicial/religious-based agents became one of the most important components of the monitoring mechanism. The abandonment of the timar institution in favor of the tax-farming institution deteriorated the multilateral monitoring mechanism.

The changing structure of agents prevented the State from monitoring the actions of agents through military campaigns or state officials. The only mechanisms were Ottoman courts and judicial/religious-based agents. This also entailed more problems within contractual relations. Judicial/religious-based agents started to establish collusion with not only high-ranking bureaucrats to protect their places but also provincial notables to capture shares from contractual relations. These groups of agents could affect actions taken by agents within the contractual relations. First, judicial/religious-based agents could manipulate the State by fabricating false complaints about existing agents. Once these complaints reached the State, the agent faced risks to lose its contracts. In terms of the game-theoretical perspective, judicial/religious-based agents achieved to establish subgame perfect equilibrium for their interest. Secondly, these group of agents could impose their judicial and religious power to promote an agent if this agent allocated a share from revenues of a contract.

One could argue that the differences between intended and actual durations were not sufficient to justify the role of legal structure and its agents. The changing prices of contracts, in this sense, provided further information in examining this specific issue. The main purpose of the State was to maximize its revenues in the Ottoman Empire as European rulers. The auction mechanism was one of the most common ways to achieve this goal. The competition among powerful groups entailed higher price offers for financial resources. Thus, the Ottoman Empire imposed a similar mechanism with small institutional differences.

The State had no incentive to change property rights, and the State ownership dominated the institutional structure. Furthermore, the State promoted one specific rule even if institutions did change over time. The State allowed agents to offer prices for financial resources they wanted. It did not matter whether this financial resource was operated by an agent or not. Once the State received a higher price, the rule allowed to transfer of financial resources from the existing agent to the new one. As it was given in the previous chapter, historical data established within this study, tax-farming contracts changed hands before their intended durations. More importantly, approximately 70% of these contracts were transferred to new agents with the same price or decreasing prices. This resulted probably from the fact that collusion among judicial/religious-based agents and the agents who were able to take a contract from the State.

It is the increase in prices expected from the auction system. But primary sources show that prices either remained stable or decreased during the early modern period. This indicates that the State failed to carry out efficient punishment to the agents who follow the defection strategy, or it is impossible to talk about the dominant power of the state. In either case, different groups benefit from lower bids. Current literature claims that these were guarantors who crop a share of contracts as financiers (Çizakça, 1996). However, historical data and equilibrium(s) that emerged within contractual relations indicate that there are different mechanisms. The role of the judges should be incorporated into the analysis of the economic performance of the Ottoman Empire, particularly for the early modern period.

## References

### Primary Sources

KŞS (Kütahya Court Records) 86/447, 102/510.
ÇŞS (Çirmen Town Court Records) 15/80-100, 15/103-4.
BŞS (Bolu Court Records) 836/32-85

### Secondary Sources

Barkey, K. (2008). *Empire of difference: The Ottomans in comparative perspective*. Cambridge University Press.

Bowles, S. (2004). *Microeconomics: Behavior, institutions and evolution*. Princeton University Press.

Çizakça, M. (1993). Tax-farming and financial decentralization in the Ottoman economy: 1520–1697. *The Journal of European Economic History, 22*(2), 219–250.

Çizakça, M. (1996). *A comparative evolution of business partnerships: The Islamic world and Europe, with specific reference to the Ottoman archives*. E. J. Brill.

Darling, L. (1996). *Revenue-raising and legitimacy: Tax collecting and finance administration in the Ottoman Empire, 1560–1660*. E. J. Brill.

Karaman, K. K., & Pamuk, Ş. (2010). Ottoman state finances in European perspective. *The Journal of Economic History, 70*(3), 593–629.

Kuran, T. (2005). The logic of financial westernization in the Middle East. *Journal of Economic Behavior and Organization, 56*, 593–615.

Ma, D., & Rubin, J. (2019). The paradox of power: Principal agent problems and administrative capacity in imperial China (and other absolutist regimes). *Journal of Comparative Economics, 47*(2), 277–294.

Nagata, Y. (1999). *Muhsinzade Mehmed Paşa ve Ayanlık Müessesesi*. Akademi Kitabevi

Pamuk, Ş. (2004a). The evolution of Ottoman financial institutions, 1600–1914. *Financial History Review, 11*(1), 7–32.

Pamuk, Ş. (2004b). Institutional Change and the Longevity of the Ottoman Empire, 1500–1800. *The Journal of Interdisciplinary History, 35*(2), 225–247.

Pamuk, Ş. (2009). Changes in factor markets in the Ottoman Empire 1500–1800. *Continuity and Change, 24*(1), 1–30.

Root, H. L. (1989). Tying the king's hands: Credible commitment and royal fiscal policy during the old regime. *Rationality and Society, 1*(2), 240–258.

Salzmann, A. (1993). An ancien regime revisited: "Privatization" and political economy in the eighteenth-century Ottoman Empire. *Politics & Society, 21*(4), 393–423.

Salzmann, A. (2004). *Tocqueville in the Ottoman Empire: Rival paths to the modern state*. E. J. Brill.

Van Bavel, B. (2015). History as laboratory to better understand the formation of institutions. *The Journal of Institutional Economics, 11*(1), 69–91.

Yaycioglu, A. (2016). *Partners of the Empire, the crisis of the Ottoman order in the age of revolutions*. Stanford University Press.

CHAPTER 8

# An Assessment Over Previous Chapters and Concluding Remarks

**Abstract** This chapter includes two different parts. First, it examines each chapter in brief. Secondly, a general discussion is given on why the institutional structure of the Ottoman Empire caused failures through presented arguments in previous chapters. The findings and arguments of this study have provided a contribution to the early modern Ottoman Empire in different ways. First, institutional change should be considered as a cause of long-run divergence in comparison with European societies. Secondly, the argument of the recent literature over coercive power of the central authority in contractual relations is inadequate in explaining the failure in contractual relations. If this argument is valid, then the prices of contracts would be in an increasing trend in the long term. The failure, in this sense, has emerged from the role of judicial/religious-based agents and their efforts to protect their interests within the institutional environment. Consequently, the divergence should be examined through economic institutions as well as non-economic institutions, particularly during the early modern period.

**Keywords** The Ottoman Empire · Institutions · The structure of law · Judicial decisions · Divergence



B. Altay and F. Oğuz, *Rules, Contracts and Law Enforcement in the Ottoman Empire*, Palgrave Studies in Institutions, Economics and Law, https://doi.org/10.1007/978-3-030-79577-1_8

In the last few decades, there is growing literature on the role of institutions on economic performance. Several Ottoman economic historians have started to give careful attention to the relationship between institutions and changing economic and political structures. These studies, however, mostly have presented implicit analyses, and a few have developed theoretical arguments over why the revenue extracting institution failed over time. The lack of data has made it difficult for Ottoman economic historians to establish an explicit and systematic approach on revenue extracting institutions and their effects on economic performances for the early modern period. This study is based on archives on contractual relations and uses modern game theory to get a better understanding of the Ottoman economic institutions in the case of tax-farming contracts.

The Ottoman archives contain tax-farming contracts only sporadically. More importantly, limited primary sources have prevented researchers from incorporating the role of legal institutions and mechanisms into the analysis. We offer a systematic and analytic perspective on the role of economic and non-economic institutions and economic performances of the Ottoman Empire in the early modern period. The recent literature, in this sense, has overlooked the role of legal institutions in contractual relations. The theoretical literature has offered doorstep conditions, but the recent literature has overlooked the question of why the Ottoman Empire could not establish the rule of law even if doorstep conditions emerged within the institutional environment? Therefore, this study has examined the relationship between the legal institutions and the economic performance of the Ottoman Empire through tax-farming contracts. Our analysis is based on a theoretical background.

Our findings on the relationship between legal and economic structure have been presented explicitly through a game-theoretical model. The findings have shown that the Ottoman Empire failed to establish the rule of law, and the divergence with European societies started to enhance during the early modern period. A long-standing presumption in this literature has been that the divergence has a marked increase between the center (Europe) and periphery during the industrialization. The results have suggested that institutional differences have fostered the divergence where societies mostly employed similar institutional structures but different mechanisms during the early modern period.

The early modern period has been characterized by contractual relations between the rulers (kings, lords, princes, sultans, etc.) and powerful groups. The cooperation among contracting parties has been a major driving force of economic progress. Cooperative solutions have supported Pareto optimum outcomes rather than other equilibrium(s) with lower payoffs. The theoretical background based on the rule of law context has included historical and institutional literature. This literature has been crucial to understanding how some societies solved credible commitment and the law enforcement problems and how others failed over time. Furthermore, the literature has presented how institutions did change over time. The theoretical background has shown that the Ottoman Empire developed institutions, and these institutions emerged for the same purpose under the rules of the game. We have shown that institutional change that emerged in the Ottoman Empire is compatible with collective action theories.

The following parts have presented compliance of Ottoman institutions and the rule of law perspective (Chapter 3). This chapter has focused on how the Ottoman Empire developed contractual relations in the first place. Historical perspectives have shown that the powerful leaders of the Ottoman Empire established contractual relations with powerful groups within the society. As it can be expected that the sultans chose to allocate certain economic and political privileges toward powerful groups in exchange for collecting taxes and providing military troops in favor of the central authority. Thus, this chapter has forged a link between the theoretical background and historical perspective for the contractual relations that emerged in the Ottoman Empire. To show this relationship in a measurable way, this study has focused on the NWW approach. The doorstep conditions of this approach on the way to the rule of law have been traceable through the data extracted from tax-farming contracts. Thus, this relationship among theoretical and historical backgrounds has shown that the rule of law for elites was established within the institutional environment of the Ottoman Empire. On the other side, the arguments presented have suggested that rapid territorial expansion deteriorated law enforcement due to the increasing transaction costs that emerged from exogenous shocks and endogenous dynamics.

This study has shown the importance of tax-farming institutions within the economic structure. The recent literature has had a common agreement on the role of revenue extracting institutions during the early modern period. The detailed presentation of economic variables in a comparative perspective has provided a better understanding of how economic and non-economic institutions and their changes affected the economic performance of the Ottoman Empire over time. The data have suggested that the divergence emerged in not only per capita GDP levels but also revenue extracting abilities during the early modern period. This divergence has formed the main question of this study: what was the role of legal institutions in the failure of the Ottoman Empire, particularly during the eighteenth century?

This study has also incorporated the structure of law and the role of judicial/religious-based agents into the analysis. The historical perspective has suggested that judges (*kadis*) did not have the right to participate in contractual relations. Recent literature has argued that judges were responsible for executing auctions and approving entitlements (*berats)* of the highest bidder agents. One of the main contributions of this study is based on the role of judges in contractual relations. Even if a few researchers have focused on the actions taken by judges within the institutional environment, these studies have overlooked the problem of why the perception of these groups of agents changed and how these groups achieved to determine the path of institutional change to protect their interests. This chapter has suggested that judges played a crucial role in the emergence of the rule of law for elites. Another important institutional mechanism that the recent literature overlooked is that the central authority had the power to assign judges toward Sharia Courts. As it has been given, once a dispute emerged in contractual relations, judges had a strong incentive to make their decisions in favor of the central authority. The findings have shown that agents had two options; first, they could establish collusion with the judges by transferring a certain share from tax revenues, and secondly, they chose to behave opportunistically. This chapter has presented the rules of the game given in contracts. It has been suggested that the rules allowed the judges to exploit contractual relations by deteriorating monitoring mechanisms. The rules have also suggested that judges had the power to manipulate judicial decisions to the detriment of agents to capture a certain share from tax revenues. Finally, the arguments of this chapter have presented that judges had the strong incentive to keep the existing institutional structure as they are to keep their interests through judicial transactions and the power of Sharia Courts.

Finally, this study has shed light on the structure of law and inefficient law enforcement through a descriptive analysis of tax-farming contracts. This study has employed two different variables from tax-farming contracts. The differences between intended and actual durations have formed first explicit data in examining the failure of the contractual relations. The findings have shown that a substantial proportion of tax-farming contracts had been terminated before the intended duration due to the exogenous shocks and endogenous dynamics. The theoretical background has suggested that deteriorated monitoring mechanisms and partial institutional change entailed commitment problems in contractual relations. Changing rules have been inadequate to solve commitment problems. The motivation of the central authority in maximizing revenues through auction mechanisms has directed agents to transfer their financial resources toward tax-farming contracts. The findings have also suggested that agents were mostly willing to take tax-farming contracts for political privileges. In sum, collusion among high-ranking bureaucrats of the central authority and agents has entailed contracts to change hands frequently. The second explicit data employed within this study have supported the assumptions over the differences between intended and actual durations. Our sample has presented that only 1/3 of tax-farming contracts had increasing prices during the auctions. In other words, the central authority had been able to increase its revenues from 1/3 of tax-farming contracts. The prices of other contracts have remained at the same level or decreased during the auctions. The recent literature has overlooked these two economic data that emerged from tax-farming contracts. The literature has considered this problem as a loss of state revenues in the long run. This study, however, has suggested that the rule of law for elites emerged within the institutional environment, and the judges played a crucial role in establishing this through judicial bias. This study has also shown that the judges had enough motivation to promote the rule of law for elites. If powerful groups had dominated the contract market under limited competition, judges had the chance to protect their interests through Sharia Courts.

Finally, we have offered a quantitative analysis with game-theoretical perspectives. The game theory has allowed us to examine contractual relations and the sensitivity of the outcomes regarding the rules and institutions. In this sense, game theory has enabled us to determine two main strategies of contracting parties within the rules of the game. As given in the game-theoretical model, contracting parties had two dominant strategies: cooperate or defect. The cooperation of agents is based on their choices: invest or not invest. The central authority, on the other side, has two strategies: honor and not honor the contract. The game-theoretical model has suggested that once a contractual arrangement emerged between the central authority and the agent, the strategies of contracting parties were mostly defection. Thus, a Nash Equilibrium(s) has emerged within the institutional environment. Game theory has argued that Nash equilibrium(s) is Pareto inferior, and the Pareto optimum outcomes are based on cooperation among contracting parties. The game-theoretical model has suggested that the Ottoman Empire got stuck in Nash equilibrium. The main reason is that selective and partial institutional change entailed failure to establish a competitive structure within the institutional environment. The structure of law and the role of judicial/religious-based agents had limited the institutional change to protect their interests in contractual relations. In terms of the rule of law, this study has argued that the Ottoman Empire became a typical example of a "limited access order". The structure of law and its judges, however, had prevented agents from developing mechanisms in limiting the coercive power of the central authority. The judicial/religious-based agents had used their influence to maintain the institutional structure as it did. Consequently, this study has suggested that Nash equilibrium(s) and "limited access order" survived as an inheritance in institutional change during the early modern period.

The findings and arguments of this study have contributed to the early modern Ottoman Empire in different ways. First, institutional change should be considered as a cause of long-run divergence in comparison with European societies. Secondly, the argument of the recent literature over coercive power of the central authority in contractual relations is inadequate in explaining the failure in contractual relations. If this argument is valid, then the prices of contracts would be in an increasing trend in the long term. The failure, in this sense, has emerged from the role of judicial/religious-based agents and their efforts to protect their interests within the institutional environment. Consequently, the divergence should be examined through economic institutions as well as non-economic institutions, particularly during the early modern period.

# Index






B. Altay and F. Oğuz, *Rules, Contracts and Law Enforcement in the Ottoman Empire*, Palgrave Studies in Institutions, Economics and Law, https://doi.org/10.1007/978-3-030-79577-1

The manufacturer's authorised representative in the EU is Springer Nature Customer Service Centre GmbH, Europaplatz 3, 69115 Heidelberg, Germany. If you have any concerns regarding our products, please contact ProductSafety@springernature.com

Printed and bound by CPI Group (UK) Ltd, Croydon, CR0 4YY
30/09/2026
02225466-0004